Teens Ask Deepak: All the Right Questions

by Deepak Chopra

SIMON PULSE

New York London Toronto Sydney

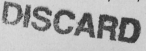

To all the teenagers today and tomorrow,
upon whom the fate of the world depends

ACKNOWLEDGMENTS

To the entire Chopra Center Staff for their loving support and
for making every bit of knowledge a reality in the life of
those who visit the center. To my personal staff, Carolyn
Rangel, Felicia Rangel, James Rangel, and Gabriela Rangel,
and to my family for their loving support.

ALSO BY DEEPAK CHOPRA
Fire in the Heart: A Spiritual Guide for Teens

SIMON & SCHUSTER
1230 Avenue of the Americas, New York, NY 10020
Text copyright © 2006 by Deepak Chopra
Illustrations copyright © 2006 by Damien Barchowsky
All rights reserved, including the right of reproduction in whole or in part in any form.
Designed by Greg Stadnyk
The text of this book is set in Rotis.
The illustrations are rendered in ink and ink wash.
Manufactured in the United States of America
First Simon & Schuster edition January 2006
10 9 8 7 6 5 4 3 2 1
Library of Congress Control Number 2005928334
ISBN-13: 978-0-689-86218-2
ISBN-10: 0-689-86218-0

CONTENTS

Introduction
Asking All the Right Questions 1

1
How Spirit Works
(. . . And It Does Work) 4

2
Success
"What's the Secret of Being Really Successful?" 42

3
Well–Being
"How Do I Find True Happiness?" 71

4
Relationships
"How Do I Fit In? Where Will I Find Love?" 124

5
God
"Does God Really Exist? How Can I Be Sure?" 162

Postscript
For Ever and Ever 202

Every child that is born is proof that God
has not yet given up on human beings.
—Rabindranath Tagore

Asking All the Right Questions

Turn on the TV any day of the week. What do you see? Teens glued to a video game or hanging out in shopping malls. Teens who hate school and make fun of anyone who is different from them. And when they try to be funny, teens come off as too smart for their teachers and too cool for their parents.

In other words, they have no soul.

But my experience tells a very different story. Teenagers worry about their souls more than any other group. Life is a riddle they are eager to solve but also feel troubled by. Teens really want to know who they are. They are old enough not to accept the stories given to children when the big questions come up:

Where's my life going?

Does God really exist?

Why does he allow so many bad things to happen?

Do I matter?

How am I ever going to make a difference?

Since you are a teenager holding this book in your hands, all these questions have run through your mind at some time. But I bet that since you first asked them, somewhere back in your childhood, most of the answers you received aren't that helpful anymore.

This isn't a book about Grandma going to heaven when she dies or God frowning down on you when you swipe cookies from the cookie jar. Whenever I talk with teenagers, they report having heard things like this as a child. They discovered something that's very true: Adults squirm when the big questions come up, especially the big spiritual ones. They don't want their kids to worry, so they give answers that all say one thing: "Don't worry. It's all okay."

And yet the big questions still keep coming up. At every age we all need to know what life is really all about. Not just on the surface, but deep down.

Teenagers are no exception. They deserve a spiritual life all their own. One that offers the kind of comfort we hope to give our children, but is different at the same time. More full of ideas. More mature. More fitting for the whole wide future that lies ahead.

That's what I've tried to do in this book, as fully and as honestly as possible. Not all the answers are nice answers. Does God let bad things happen? Yes; not always, but quite a lot of the time. Does that mean he is cruel? No, but you're really going to have to think, because a person who sits back and lets bad things happen is often cruel. Why is God different from a person, then? Let's talk about it.

That's the kind of discussion you are going to find in these pages—challenging but not delivered in big words or nice thoughts that aren't really all true. It's based on the questions teenagers actually ask me. Some were asked in person, at public talks. Others were asked around the dinner table, because my son and daughter, Gotham and Mallika, were full of questions when they were teenagers (they're now adults and happily married, with families of their own). The remaining questions were submitted over the Internet, where a Web site was set up to invite teenagers to ask anything they wanted to know about spirituality.

So here it is, the thing you asked for. Not just answers to the big questions, but a guide to spirit as seen through the eyes of teenagers, a special group in society that deserves a spiritual life different from anyone's before or since. I salute your uniqueness and invite you to read on.

How Spirit Works

(. . . AND IT DOES WORK)

I was shuffling through a pile of questions that teenagers had asked, and one popped to the surface. It's so easy to answer, and yet it's so important that I knew I had to begin with this one.

Dear Deepak,
   If you could change one thing about the history of our Earth, what would it be?

That question came from a fourteen-year-old boy. Now, what if you asked it, not to me, but to yourself? There's a lot of changes you might wish for. You might wish that nobody had discovered gunpowder, since that led to such an enormous increase in terrible wars. You might wish that medicine had discovered cures for diseases centuries ago, or that every baby who had ever been born survived to lead a productive life.

But my answer would be different. When it comes down to one and only one choice, here is mine: I wish everyone knew from birth that they had a soul.

You might not think that's much of a change. Doesn't everyone already know they have a soul? Certainly everyone—or nearly everyone—is *told* that they have a soul. But being told and knowing are two different things.

If you truly knew you had a soul, you could change the world. Which is what I'm inviting you to do. The world is changed from the inside. All the greatest people you can think of became great from the inside. Albert Einstein became great by dreaming in a new way about time and space. Leonardo da Vinci became great by imagining inventions that did not come to pass for hundreds of years (did you know that he sketched a helicopter four hundred years before the Wright brothers learned to fly?) and by having a vision of a new way to paint.

Yet there is a kind of greatness open to you right now, even if you think you are a very ordinary, average person. It's the greatness of living from your soul. What does that mean?

LIVING FROM THE SOUL

Imagine that you could have a thought and it would come true.

Imagine that you could feel safe and at peace, no matter what happened around you.

Imagine that you could love yourself as much as you wanted others to love you—and more.

Imagine that you could wake up every day to greet a new world.

Imagine that you could feel the presence of God.

Anyone who achieved these things would be considered a great success in life. I'm pretty sure that, as a teenager, you worry about how to make a good life for yourself. It can seem like an incredibly difficult project. But if all those things I asked you to imagine came true, wouldn't that be real success? Living from the level of the soul isn't about being goody-goody and hoping that God notices and smiles down on you. It's about the best kind of life you can possibly lead.

One fifteen-year-old boy asked a really important, basic question:

Dear Deepak,
What is the difference between religion and spirituality?

To me, they don't have to be different at all. To be religious and spiritual can and should be the same thing. But we have to be real here, and religion almost always means a traditional faith like Christianity or Islam or Judaism. It's practiced in groups. It takes place in churches or mosques or synagogues. There is a given set of beliefs, along with priests, scriptures, and services.

Spirituality, on the other hand, doesn't need a group. It is done one person at a time, almost always in private. I think every spiritual person reads inspiring scriptures, often from many different religious traditions. Such a person may or may not go to church. They may or may not know the set of beliefs that guide the faithful. So you can be deeply spiritual and yet not be a "good" Catholic, Jew, or Muslim. This book isn't about religion. It's about the spiritual side, the private life of the soul.

A Spiritual Quiz

Q: I think I am spiritual, but I'm not sure, especially when things start going wrong. Then I feel really alone. I'm all by myself, still struggling.

A: I think what makes spirit real is change. Spirit changes you, and when the change is very big, it can be called a transformation. Fairy tales are about a child's deep wish to be changed: Frogs transform into princes, ugly ducklings transform into swans. The amazing thing about human nature is that we are the only creatures on Earth who can transform ourselves just because we want to. A caterpillar has no choice but to be reborn as a butterfly. You do have a choice.

Here's a quiz to show you just how many things in your life—things you probably take for granted—could be transformed. Then you can see in advance what spirit could be doing for you right now.

What Can Spirit Do for You?

Directions:
Put a check ✔ beside each sentence that you agree with most of the time. Then score yourself (25 points maximum) by counting up the total number of checks.

☐ I worry about what my body looks like.

☐ What others think about my body is important.

☐ If I had a better body, people would like me more.

☐ I should work hard to get a better body.

☐ It's always better to have more money.

☐ If you don't have money, you won't be able to lead a good life.

☐ My personality bothers people, and I wish it didn't.

☐ Being supported by others is really important to me.

☐ Going against the group doesn't pay. People will laugh at you or put you down.

☐ If I can buy what I want and do the things I like to do, I am happy.

☐ The most important thing is to look out for yourself, because no one else will.

☐ When bad things happen, they could be a punishment from God.

☐ The world is unsafe. It's really important to be on your guard.

☐ I like retreating into fantasy, such as seeing myself as a rich and famous rock star or a celebrity.

☐ When you really look at life, it isn't fair.

☐ When I think of the word *powerful*, it doesn't apply to me.

☐ I often have a hard time getting motivated.

☐ I'm not sure what I really believe in.

☐ I don't think I really have a vision of my own life.

☐ Secretly there are people I look down upon. I know that I am better than them.

☐ If someone likes me, I like them back. If they don't like me, I dislike them, too.

☐ I am afraid of death.

☐ I get bored easily, especially if no one is paying attention to me.

☐ I have to get what I want, and I make pretty sure that I do.

☐ If you ask me what I am proudest of, it's all the cool things I have, like my PlayStation or my family's house and car.

☐ Total score

RATINGS
0–10 points

You are spiritually mature for your age. Compared with most teens, you don't feel insecure and you don't depend so much on externals such as approval from others. You have a sense that outer things like money and popularity aren't all-important. Your sense of security will be an excellent foundation for the spiritual journey that lies ahead.

11–20 points

Spirit can do a lot to make you feel more secure and happy. Right now you depend a lot on conforming to the group and making sure that your life has comfortable things in it. Body image is important to you because you don't want to look different, and secretly you wish you were perfect. You look upon externals as important because almost everyone you know believes this too.

21–25 points

You are very hungry for spirit, even though you might not know this yet. What you do know is that you are frightened that you don't fit in. Group pressure hasn't helped, because you want to be approved of so much that any kind of negative reaction makes you miserable. In your fantasies you'd like to have as much money, fame, and success as possible because you don't really see any other route to happiness. For you, contact with your soul will bring much more security and peace of mind if you stick with the spiritual journey and don't get discouraged.

After taking this quiz, you might ask, "What was spiritual about these questions? You didn't even mention the soul, and God came up only once." I didn't mention spirit because, to me, being spiritual is about knowing yourself and finding the deep secrets of happiness. The more you look for happiness in external things, the farther you are from your soul. Being a teenager brings all kinds of peer pressure, and for most people, adapting to the group sets the stage for the rest of their adult life. However, this is also a great age to learn to turn inward and find out what's really going on inside you.

There was a famous medical study in which thousands of Harvard graduates were followed from college onward until they reached fifty and beyond. The study wanted to find out the reasons that men get so many premature heart attacks (the study began in the 1950s, when the epidemic of heart attacks was highest in this country).

You might think that heart attacks strike people who are the most stressed, who eat a bad diet, or who have a history of heart disease in their family. Those factors certainly do contribute. But the surprising fact is that in this study the number one risk was none of these. It was whether the person had taken time to really look at himself. Men who faced their inner conflicts and problems very early, in their twenties, were least likely to have a heart attack.

Men who avoided looking inward had the most heart attacks.

This study made a big impression on me when I started out as a doctor, because I saw that something invisible made a huge difference in people's bodies. Thoughts were killing people, if you really come down to it, while changing those thoughts helped their hearts to remain alive. That's a big clue to why the spiritual life is actually the best life you can lead, even on the physical level.

God for a Day

Q: If you could be God for a day, would you?

A: When you live from your soul, you are coming as close as you can to being God. And not just for a day. Your soul is permanent. It is always with you, always urging you to become more than you think you can be. Of course no one can actually be God—I have a hard time even imagining what it would be like to be God for a day. God is infinite, and I can't imagine being infinite. God knows everything at once. God is beyond time. God is in every atom of creation. I can't imagine those things either.

But I can imagine touching my soul with my mind and my heart. When I do that, my small speck of God is present with me. Then I don't have to fall back on imagining—I can have a spiritual life for real. And so can you.

Most people don't realize this because they don't really know their own soul. First of all, your soul is invisible.

You know you have a face and hands and that they are attached to a body. No one has to tell you those things. You know you have feelings, even though they are invisible, and thoughts in your head. No one has to tell you about those, either.

SLEEPY SOULS

Many people go through life as if they don't know they have a soul. Somebody told them they did, but it didn't sink in. Or not

very deeply. In these cases, the soul grew sleepy; it drifted off into a kind of never-never land, where it still lives. You can't see it because it's too far away. You can't visit it or listen in on it, because wherever this never-never land is, nobody knows how to get there. So basically the soul is a nice story, and when things get really rough, you can always fall back on this strange, invisible thing called your soul, which is your connection to God. (And to be really honest, does he seem to be any closer? God, too, lives in an invisible place far away from Earth, although we all were told in childhood that when you die, you will go to that place to meet him. Or her. Let's be fair and give God a chance to be either a he or a she—or maybe both.)

I want to clear up this mystery and bring the soul back down to Earth. If I could imagine changing the history of the world, that's the change I would have made long, long ago. (Although I must admit that half the fun is searching for your soul, so perhaps the world was created perfectly just the way it is.)

The fact that you are reading this book means that you are already searching for answers and seeking your soul. You are into the mystery. You are excited, I hope, by the chase. Let's chase together, because at your side I can show you how spirit works here and now.

If you know about that, you will have a huge advantage, not just in the spiritual chase, but in the game of life.

SPIRIT WORKS

To me, that's always number one. If you ask me whether angels are real, for example, I will give you my personal opinion, but I will also step outside my personal opinion to give you an answer that will work for you.

These answers will make you think on your own.

These answers will be honest. If I don't know how to solve a problem, I will tell you so.

These answers will open a door.

An open door is what everyone really needs. Unless I open a door into your own life, what good is this book? Concerning angels, anybody can say, "Sure, angels exist." Or they can say the opposite: "Angels are a nice story that you can believe in if you want to, like the tooth fairy." One answer is yes, the other is no. But neither one will really do you much good. You already know in advance that some people believe in angels, while others don't.

However, if I can open a door in your mind, you might just meet an angel one day. Or you might explore your desire to meet one so deeply that it will bring you great peace. Or a vision. Or a road to heaven. I don't know exactly where your doors will lead to, but I do know that you need to have as many open doors as possible.

AN ANGEL STORY

I do have a good angel story, though. Right after World War I there was an old village priest in France. He was much beloved by all the villagers, who considered him very holy and very brave. You see, he had gone into the trenches with the common soldiers in the heat of battle so that he could pray with them. Sometimes he had to deliver the last rites to the young fighters, who were no older than teenagers, many of them.

One day the priest got caught in an attack of mustard gas, a poison that drifted through the air and did terrible damage to any part of the body that it touched. The gas touched the priest's eyes, and he lost much of his sight.

So now it's several years after the war, and the priest is walking down a dusty country road. Suddenly a bicycle comes speeding around the corner, moving very fast. There's no time for the priest to jump aside, and he can't see well enough to know that he's about to be hit.

All at once a stranger appears from nowhere and lifts the bicycle, rider and all, out of the road. He gently sets it down on the shoulder of the road and walks away. The cyclist can't believe what just happened, and he reports in the village that this was a genuine miracle: The stranger who appeared out of nowhere was an angel. But the old priest, who accepts the story of what happened, never gives an opinion one way or another. Was it an angel? Was it a miracle? The old priest never said.

But I think the priest would have smiled at a saying from Albert Einstein, who pointed out that there are only two ways to look at the world: Either nothing in the universe is a miracle, or everything is.

I want to show you how to see the second way.

The Greatest Miracle

Q: If everything is a miracle, why haven't I ever seen a real one?

A: You have; you just didn't notice it. A miracle is going on right before your eyes. In fact, it is the greatest miracle. It's you. You will never see any kind of miracle until you begin to see this one first. Let's take a short trip into outer space. Step out into your backyard any night and look up at the sky. The bright wash of stars that sweeps across the sky, looking like a broad ribbon, is the Milky Way, our galaxy. It contains billions of stars, and although they look close together to your naked eye, in fact each one is many light-years away from the other.

YOUR BODY IS A MIRACLE

Now consider this: Your body contains a thousand cells for each star in the Milky Way galaxy. But instead of floating in space like stars, these trillions of cells are talking to one another. They know exactly what every other cell is doing. Billions of messages shoot through your nervous system, your bloodstream, and everywhere else in your body. You cannot take a breath of air into your lungs without its being known by your brain, your liver, even the tiniest blood cell far away in your little toe.

That's only the beginning of the miracle. Right now your brain is reading these words (it is also doing hundreds of other things simultaneously, but we can talk about only one miracle at a time). Your brain uses only one basic food to do everything it does, a food called glucose, or blood sugar. Now, blood sugar isn't that different from the white sugar in your kitchen cabinet. Take that bag of sugar off the shelf and ask it to think. Ask it to read a book or fall in love. It can't, no matter how long you wait. How did blood sugar learn to fall in love? It cannot be explained. The miracle of your body encloses many, many other miracles.

Just so that you are convinced, let me give another amazing example. The elements sodium and chlorine are very nasty stuff.

Sodium is extremely poisonous, and chlorine is such a toxic gas that taking just a whiff of it would immediately start to kill the cells in the nose. Yet when sodium and chlorine are combined, what do you get? Salt, a chemical totally necessary to life itself. Now, how did two radical poisons ever get together to make life? No one can explain it.

THE GREATEST MIRACLE

Here you sit, then, the greatest miracle in existence. I could go on and on about your miraculousness. Nobody can explain how your DNA learned to divide and duplicate itself. I'm sure you already know that this happens, since a baby is formed when one fertilized cell in the mother's womb divides over and over to produce the billions of cells in a newborn infant. No other chemical can divide to duplicate itself. For at least ten billion years after the big bang the universe rolled along, perfectly content with gases and liquids and solids that never duplicated even one atom. Yet DNA, which has billions of tiny connected parts, duplicates itself every second inside you.

If you are the greatest miracle, then it's not too much for you to ask for more miracles. That's really how spirituality works. You

notice one miracle, and it leads you on a trail hunting for more. The trip starts by sitting down and realizing that you are a miracle. If you ever forget that fact, go back to it. Remind yourself over and over. Because walking the trail of miracles isn't always easy. It has lots of ups and downs. Yet no matter how twisty or confusing life becomes, your own personal miracle keeps going, in billions and billions of cells. You are living proof that miracles exist. That's a wonderful thing to remember at any age.

Flipping the Switch

Q: Why don't I feel like I am a miracle?

A: You don't feel like a miracle because you haven't flipped the spiritual switch yet. Life is choices, and some people spend year after year not flipping the switch. Therefore, they're not seeing any miracles at all. Imagine a dark room at night. You walk in, but you can't see a thing. So you flip the light switch, and now the things that were in darkness can be seen. Yet what did you actually do? That little switch on the wall is connected to a power plant far away. Enormous energy is generated in the plant, all controlled by the flick of a finger. Without the switch you would never know that you could tap into such a huge supply of energy.

Spiritual power is like electricity; it can run a lot of things. But unlike electricity, the power isn't physical. It comes from the soul. Or if you like, you can say that the power begins with God or spirit itself. I don't care which word you use—they are all good ones. The key thing is to decide to flip the switch. That's the only way to see the miracles that you could be doing.

The Power Source

Q: What kind of power is spiritual power?

A: This is a huge question, because spiritual power is everywhere. It goes unnoticed because in a way it's hidden behind a screen. Spirit seems to like to hide itself, yet it also likes to show itself too. To make it come out of hiding, you have to begin to pay attention to a different part of life. I already mentioned that the blood sugar in your brain is not all that different from the white sugar you buy at the store. But I didn't tell you what that difference actually is. Blood sugar has spiritual power in it. In fact, all the atoms and molecules in your body contain the same spiritual power, so let's look at them a little more.

A MYSTERY IN EVERY BREATH

Let's look at air. The air around you is quite amazing. When you take in your next breath, you will be breathing in atoms that someone in China breathed out a few days ago. With each breath you will be taking in several million atoms breathed out by Jesus Christ and Buddha. But even more amazing is this: When you breathe in an atom of oxygen, it is invisibly filled with spiritual power. The atom starts out as a dead, random bit of matter floating around the world. Yet the instant it enters your lungs, it becomes alive. It attaches itself to a red blood cell and gets to work. Three seconds later it could be powering your heart or fueling a thought or doing thousands of other jobs.

Life happens incredibly fast. Your cells have only three seconds of oxygen inside them, so this little oxygen atom has to race where it's needed, and when it arrives, it has to know exactly what to do. A fireman putting out a fire is working very slowly compared with the oxygen in your blood, which has to slip into a cell, where millions and millions of other atoms are working at top speed, linked together in astoundingly complicated tasks—so complicated that I can't stop to describe them except to say that a high-speed computer is about a million times simpler.

The fantastic voyage of one oxygen atom takes place on a

supersmall scale, yet the power of the universe is at work here. And what is the universe's power all about? Exactly what you are about:

Life Growth Intelligence

These three things shape the grand plan of the universe. When oxygen floats around in the air, you can't see that it's part of the universe's grand plan, but the instant that oxygen gets inside you, the plan fires up and gets going. Your body is nothing but a huge storm of life, growth, and intelligence. Every single process in it serves the grand plan, and so does every other miracle you can name.

Life rushes forward like a huge river, tumbling over obstacles, shaping the landscape, filling up the empty places, conquering death every inch of the way.

Growth brings new things into existence, turns random matter into incredible shapes, blossoms into dreams that come true, and turns a primitive universe of swirling gases into amazing, complicated forms, no two ever exactly alike.

Intelligence invents what is going on and imagines unknown stories that come true before your very eyes.

If you want to be part of the universe's grand plan, these three things are where you will get your power.

The *power of life* is waiting to be ever more alive and fresh and ready to speed you on your way.

The *power of growth* is ready to unfold new regions of creation that are sleeping until you wake them up.

The *power of intelligence* is waiting for your next idea, dream, or wish. These are invisible things, but spirit has placed them in your hands. You can flip the switch and get all this power to flow through you. Unlimited power. The power that lights up the stars even as it lights up your life.

Finding Your Power

Q: Where is this switch you're talking about?

A: In you, of course. There's no other place it could be. There's a wonderful old poem by Kabir, who lived in India many centuries ago but is still revered today. He says, "I visited the wisest men but didn't find God there. I read all the sacred books but didn't find God there. I bathed in the holy rivers and traveled to the most ancient temples, yet nowhere did I find God, until one day I opened the door in my own heart, and what a surprise! There was God waiting for me with a smile."

You'll find the same search in every religious tradition—and the same answer being given. The switch you have to flip is in your own heart. We could also say it is in your mind, because spirit doesn't have just one home. The three powers of life, growth, and intelligence flow through every particle of you (every particle of this world, too).

So the good news is that spirit isn't going anywhere. You'll never lose out on it. You'll never misplace your portion of the universe's power or accidentally be left out of the cosmic plan.

The trick is that all this power lies at the source, not on the surface. Mighty rivers flow from a tiny source in the mountains; where the Mississippi River begins there's a place so narrow you can walk across it with one step. So don't worry that your source is small. At the source you already possess far more spiritual power than you can imagine. Enough to create a world. Enough to transform you. Enough to solve your deepest worries and bring about your most cherished hopes.

HUNTING FOR THE UNICORN

Have you ever thought much about the unicorn, that mythical beast that is imagined as a flashing white horse with a single horn in its forehead? In the Middle Ages many artists made paintings and tapestries describing the hunt for the unicorn. It wasn't an actual animal, but a symbol for Christ or God or the soul. The tapestries and paintings showed the unicorn running through the woods, but it was understood that this mythical beast actually lived inside each person.

The unicorn is still alive, and it still lives where it always has. You and I are going on our own personal unicorn hunt. It may take a whole book to turn you into a good hunter, but I've already shown you how the hunt begins:

Know that you are a miracle.

Know that you have a unique place in the cosmic plan.

Know that spiritual power is yours for the asking.

Know that the hunt is going to take you to your source, where all the power comes from.

Got all that? Good, because even if each thing doesn't seem totally true right now, you really have flipped the switch that lights up the world. We are off and running. We're not in the dark anymore.

Getting More Out of Life

Q: **Okay, I flipped the switch. How will I know that I am starting to be spiritual? I have friends who believe in God and go to church, but they aren't always the nicest kids or the ones who live the best life.**

A: Spirituality is a way to get more out of life. I connect it to power because if you don't have the power, spirituality will remain pretty thin and not very useful. Every other way to get more out of life takes place on the surface.

You've already heard, over and over, that success takes hard work. You've been told all the bad things that happen to anyone who drops out of school and "ruins their life." You've been reminded about the rules of right and wrong. You probably have even thought about getting the right social connections and making money. Preferably a lot of money.

GOING DEEPER

But spirituality isn't about any of these things. It's about going deeper into life and finding out what the big plan is, the universal plan that you play your part in. You could call this a secret voyage, because very few people know how to take it. You have to be part explorer, part psychologist, part detective. When you go on this secret voyage, only you know about it. Nothing is more exciting. Your friends who go to church aren't on this journey just because they go to church. Your friends who don't go to church aren't missing out on this journey just because they don't go to church. Everyone decides on their own, in their heart of hearts.

But one thing is for sure: Since you have spirit inside you, you are ready for this most exciting of journeys.

We've only peeked through the doorway of spirit, but already a dozen questions must be popping up in your head: How do I know God is real? How does spirit work? What good will it do me? What can I expect to happen to me if I try to be more spiritual?

I'm going to try to answer each and every question, but here are some quick answers in advance:

Is God real?
Yes, but you might be surprised how different God's reality is from what you think right now.

How does spirit work?
It works by showing you the best way to solve any challenge.

What good will it do me?
You will grow and grow all your life, and every step will bring you closer to truth.

25

THE BASICS

Spirit is the word I am using to describe the whole invisible world that lies beyond your five senses. It covers everything and is therefore the most general word we will be using. An artist who paints an inspired picture is spiritual to me, even if he doesn't care about God. A mother's love is spiritual—in fact, all love is spiritual.

The word *soul* means your own spirit, your personal spark of creation. To me, the soul is my source. Every thought, wish, desire, dream, and fantasy can be traced back to the soul. It has also been called your higher self. It's the part of you that belongs with God at all times.

God means the creator, but more than that. God is the highest and purest intelligence in the universe. He (or she) stands for all the sacred things that you will be searching for on your inner journey: truth, faith, love, inspiration, creativity. If any of these words are important to you, you are already standing at the beginning of your search for God.

What can I expect to happen to me?

You will be transformed. Even a month from now you might look in the mirror and say, "Is that really me?"

Where Am I Going?

Q: If I take this spiritual journey, where does it end? Do I get to see God? Do I become a holy person like a saint?

A: Traditionally the spiritual journey ends when you are enlightened. This isn't an easy word. When I came to America from India, the whole concept of "enlightened" did a flip-flop. In India, where I grew up, an enlightened person was like a holy saint, someone who had gone beyond all the sorrows and ignorance of normal life. To be enlightened meant you were close to God. In America, where I took my first job as a doctor, the most enlightened people were scientists. They generally looked upon spirituality as superstition, and beliefs about God were something you kept to yourself and didn't talk about.

STAGES OF THE JOURNEY

So I've thought and thought, for more than twenty years, about how to present the spiritual journey. And here's my sketch of two people who have made real spiritual progress. You can use these outlines as a kind of mirror to the ways you will change.

#1: Making Progress

The first person has really taken spirituality seriously. He (or she) started out wanting more self-knowledge. If you met him, you would immediately notice that he's not just an ordinary person. He's pretty unique. The approval of others isn't that important. He's not that impressed by money. He doesn't believe that just because you're better off, that means you're better.

Over time he has found quite a lot of inner peace. Extreme events can shake him out of this peace, but he isn't thrown off balance for long. He isn't scared by his own emotions, and when he feels a strong worry or a burst of anger, he knows that this is just a passing event. In general he has learned to love and appreciate life, both his own life and the life around him. Other people are souls equal to his, and for that he offers respect. He doesn't judge people by externals. He has found a way to forgive the wrongs done to him, and he can also forgive himself.

If you asked him what he is proud of, he would point to his vision of life and the love that has come to him.

If you asked him who he is, he would say, "I am a work in progress."

#2: A Real Master

The second person has done enough spiritual work to be truly transformed. If you met her (or him), you'd notice a strong presence of

Secure

At peace

Able to forgive

Accepting

Knowing yourself well

Loving

Following your vision

Seeing your life as successful

peace. This person feels wise. Her inner peace is rock solid. Without hesitating, she is kind to you, and after two seconds you know you can trust her completely.

She loves life and everything in it. Everyday anxiety about the world's bad state doesn't shake her belief in spirit. Somehow she has found a way to envision life as perfect. Her knowledge of human nature runs very deep, and so does her knowledge of God and spirit. She doesn't just talk about spirit; she lives it at every moment.

If you asked her what she is proudest of, she might surprise you by having no pride at all. Or she would say that she is proud to be a drop in the eternal ocean of Being.

If you asked her who she is, she would say, "I am one with everything."

These are very brief sketches, but in them I've tried to show you who you could be. Person #1 could easily be you if you really want to go on the spiritual journey. All you have to do is start making progress. Life isn't about being perfect, it's about being a little better every day. Person #1 knows this. By making a little progress every day, he (or she) has overcome a lot of the doubt and insecurity that you probably know all too well. We all know doubt and insecurity. They don't go away just with wishing. They don't get better just by growing up. You have to turn inward to find a place inside yourself that you can trust as your home and safe haven. The world around us isn't going to change automatically for the better, so you have to. Every day is a challenge, and going inward is the best way to meet those challenges. Person #1 was just like you as a teenager, but now he has learned how to change himself to meet the challenge of life.

Person #2 is someone I call a master. I could use other terms, like *sage, saint, guru*, or *enlightened one*. Those words are a bit too loaded for me, meaning that some people have negative opinions about them that they've picked up along the way. But everyone, I think, wants to be a master at something. Masters know their craft very, very well. They aren't beginners

A REAL MASTER KEY WORDS

Reverence

Unity

Being

Wisdom

In tune with everything

Totally at peace

Deep trust in God

Compassion

MAKING PROGRESS REMINDERS

A journey of a thousand miles begins with one step.

This is my journey. I can travel it at my own speed.

My soul is always with me.

My life is about spirit, even when it seems to be about a thousand other things.

I am a unique part of the cosmic plan. I am needed in the universe.

I am about life, growth, and intelligence. Every day I can acquire a little more of each.

The greatest person on Earth may be a huge bonfire compared with my little candle, but both are made from the same light.

anymore. They have experience and skill under their belt. If that appeals to you, why not take it a step further and be a master of your own self? Person #2 has done that. She has gone into the light and discovered her true home. She may never say the word *God,* but she has a deep reverence for all of creation. Hers is a blessed life, and my own life's journey is modeled on such visionaries. They are like the older, wiser brothers and sisters of humanity. I hope you are fortunate enough to meet such a person, because once you do, you will never forget them. Masters have a presence that is truly astonishing. But they aren't aliens. They don't come from another planet. They are the result of the transformation that you are about to begin at this very moment. Which means mastery could be in your future too.

First Steps

Q: I am excited by all these new ideas, but I admit that I am also a total beginner. What do I have to do to go on the spiritual journey?

A: There are three steps that will ignite your spirit and bring it out of hiding. They are simple steps; you don't need to be special or gifted or smart to take them.

Step #1

Notice the hints life is giving you. I am talking about unusual things that happen every day. For example, have you ever thought of somebody's name and then had that person call you on the phone a moment later? Have you had a dream that came true or said a prayer that was granted? These are hints coming from the soul, and so are the following experiences from young people:

I really love rainbows. It's like magic when one appears, and although this sounds weird, I have actually asked for a rainbow and then seen one that day.

I was looking after my baby brother when he was two. He was a real handful then—the terrible twos. But after running around, he got settled down, and when he fell asleep, I had the feeling that I was looking at an angel. I wished I could be as peaceful as he looked lying on the carpet sleeping.

Step #2

Make the spiritual clues in your life, even the tiny ones, *significant*. Pay attention. Don't turn your back on what your soul is saying. This is important because the conversation with your soul is two-way. A hint coming to you is like the soul saying, "Hello, are you there?" and when you pay attention, you are replying, "Yes, I'm here." Most people don't acknowledge their clues, which is like hanging up the phone when somebody calls you. The conversation is suddenly over.

Here are some experiences that young people did find significant:

I was hiking up in the mountains, and we came to a mountain lake. My friend and I took out our cameras to take pictures. Just at that instant all the clouds parted, and a big ray of sunshine hit the mountain lake. I had a shiver go down my spine, as if God was noticing us and smiling down.

I don't tell anybody this, but sometimes I feel as if I love everyone in the whole world.

I think I have seen a light around me, or at least I dreamed that I was in the light. It's happened only a few times, but this experience made a big impression on me.

Step #3

Value what you are experiencing. Only the things you think are valuable are really going to grow and improve. If you own a new car but let it go without an oil change or a wash, you are not giving it any value, and therefore it runs down much more quickly. If you don't value what your soul tells you, your experiences will fade away quickly. By saying to yourself, "This is important. I really want to know what my soul is saying," you are making the spiritual connection stronger every day.

Here are experiences that two young people valued:

I was playing football and it was a really tense game. A long pass came my way, and as I jumped up to catch it, I had the feeling that time slowed down. I was, like, in a slow-motion movie, and for that one moment I was sure the ball was going straight into my hands. (It did.)

I have days when I really feel like I'm walking on air. If I stepped on a scale, my body would be half as light as usual. On these days I feel I could do anything. The whole world is friendly to me. God is on my side.

HINTS FROM SPIRIT

Did any of these happen to you today?

A feeling of lightness in your body.

A streaming or flowing sensation in your body.

A sense that all is well, that you are at home in the world.

A feeling of complete peacefulness.

A feeling of landing in a soft place where you are safe.

A feeling that you are not what you seem to be, that you have been playing a part that isn't the real you.

A feeling that something lies beyond the sky or behind the mirror.

A thought that said, "I know more than I think I do."

A thought that said, "I need to find out what's real."

A thought that said, "I need to find out who I really am."

Your inner voices became very quiet.

You suddenly sensed that you were walking through a dream.

I imagine you are a bit surprised by these three steps. They don't involve anything religious. In fact, they are just new mental habits. If you are looking for a new friend, having just moved to a new town, what do you do?

You *notice* people who might be potential friends.

You put *significance* on the gestures of friendship that somebody might show you, such as helping you find a class or complimenting you on how you are dressed.

You *value* those people who are willing to accept you and take you into their circle.

Finding your soul is not that different from finding a new friend. By now you've learned my little trick, that I don't use the spiritual terms you are used to from church or Sunday school. But these three steps are very spiritual anyway, and here's why:

You are much more than you think you are. At this moment you are leading a spiritual life, only you haven't noticed it (most people don't, so that's not a failing). Your soul is always sending you hints about where your spirit wants you to go. All I want you to do is notice those hints, give them a bit of significance, and then value them. If you do that, something very surprising will happen. You will start to make friends with your soul. You will open up a channel to spirit simply by paying attention.

So, what are these hints your soul is dropping? I am going to give you a long list because I don't want to leave any out. Don't be alarmed or discouraged. I'm not asking you to notice everything on the list, much less to memorize it. My purpose is to open your eyes to how many ways spirit is trying to make contact every day.

In one way or another the greatest spiritual experiences in history are all connected to this list. I would call all of these experiences hints from the soul. They are how someone, young or old, is beginning to think, feel, and act from the level of spirit. If you are close enough to your parents or to a good friend you can be really honest with, sit down sometime and discuss the items on the list. That's valuable because these aren't experiences we tend to talk about. Around the dinner table families talk about events of the day or where they need to be in an hour or what's on television. With friends we tend to gossip or talk about school and parents. How amazing it would be if we talked instead, even once, about the state of our souls.

Naturally, that's quite a high level

You could do something without having to think about it (this is automatic action).

You sensed a greater power acting through you.

You acted out of your own truth, not what others think or say.

You got something you really wanted without having to struggle for it.

Things started coming really easily.

You stopped fighting back, and yet things worked out all right.

You sensed that your life is part of a larger plan.

You realized that you are cared for.

You realized that your life has purpose, you matter.

You sensed that random events are not random, but form a pattern.

You saw that you are unique.

You realized that life can run itself. Everything is taken care of.

You felt drawn to your center.

You realized with wonder that life is infinitely worthwhile.

of communication, so having even one of these experiences in a day is quite good. It shows that you are starting to be awake to your soul.

A DOCTOR'S STORY

I know that this list may seem very abstract, so let me make it a bit more personal. When I was a young doctor, I had time for only two things: work and family. I got up around five each morning and rushed off to the first hospital where I had patients. By eight in the morning I might have gotten to two or three more hospitals before starting to see patients in my office. At noon I usually ate at my desk because there was always a backup of patients waiting to see me; I never had time to step out and eat in a nice restaurant. Work came first. Always.

The day didn't end after the last patient walked out the door. I had to revisit the hospitals I'd gone to that morning, and so I arrived home, dead tired, around suppertime, if I was lucky. Many days I didn't get home until after dark. My wife and I dearly loved our two little babies, but it's a wonder that they even knew their daddy's face sometimes. Between work and family I didn't have a clue about the very things I put on this list. I had no spiritual life that really touched me, because there simply wasn't enough attention to go around.

Gradually that began to change. Partly because my mother was so spiritual, partly because I took an interest in spiritual books, and partly because of some x factor I don't know about, I changed. I began to notice things. The list of items I am asking you to notice all happened to me. I was getting hints from spirit all the time, and once I paid some attention to them, once I gave them significance and value, you know what happened? More and more clues came my way.

That's how it always is. What you pay attention to grows in your life. Have you known people who get angry very quickly? If you spend time around them, you'll discover very soon that they find a lot of things that set them off. Innocent, tiny things that nobody else gets angry about, such as a car parked the wrong way, a slow ticket line at the movie theater, or random remarks from strangers. Their anger is what they keep returning to, over and over, fueling it with tiny events during the day. That's the negative side of paying attention. The positive side is to notice the tiny events during the day that are hints from spirit. Other people may not notice anything unusual in their life, but if you start noticing these tiny clues, soon you will have a true spiritual life.

These Things Will Start to Grow

APPRECIATION

You'll begin to appreciate your own uniqueness, your own inner world, your own place in creation. Here is how some kids put it:

I am really starting to feel like I might be special and could lead a special life.

If I am by myself just looking around at things, I can see a lot more than before. Even just watching my dog play is different than before. I can see how really alive he is and how much he enjoys his life.

What you said about miracles is coming true for me, in that I don't see myself as just an ordinary kid anymore. I really am unique, and that means something to me.

WONDER

Instead of walking past something that could fill you with awe, whether it's a full moon, a rose, a baby's smile, or a look of love, you will begin to have a moment of wonder. Here is how some kids put it:

Everybody uses the word "awesome" all the time, so it barely means anything anymore. I am starting to see "awesome" instead of just saying it.

I saw this surf movie just because some of my friends dragged me along. I don't care about surfing, but suddenly there were shots of these mighty waves, so huge and powerful, towering over these tiny surfers. I really did feel awed by them. I began to see that life could be like that, surfing the enormous power of it everywhere around us.

ALERTNESS

You will begin to feel more awake and less dull. Everyday things won't be routine anymore. They will start to show you the spark of life that is inside everything. Here is how some kids put it:

I call it the zing. I am not just looking at stuff, but actually feel a zing, a tiny thrill, at bright colors and certain music.

In commercials they show stupid stuff like eating some kind of candy and getting a burst of excitement in your mouth. But recently I have felt this burst of excitement just because I started looking for it. Not from candy, but from something like the tropical fish in a tank. I look at them closely and keep looking, and all at once I feel very excited by this incredibly beautiful thing I am seeing.

FULLNESS

You will lose that bored, empty feeling that comes about when we take our life for granted. Instead, waking up each day will be like waking up to a new world. Each day *is* a new world, so this is a great change, a big step into a better and higher reality. Here is how some kids put it:

I have started this thing where I lie in bed when I first wake up. I close my eyes and try to feel the new day. It's like a special morning feeling. When I feel it, the day becomes this new thing and I am full of hope for what might happen.

I look for one special moment every day. It has to be a moment where something happens that never happened before. When I wasn't looking, I thought my life was mostly the same stuff every day. But actually, there is always a special moment once you open your eyes. You could say that I am on the lookout for change. I don't just see the same old things anymore.

PRESENCE

You will begin to feel the presence of spirit. It's like sensing that there's somebody behind the scenes who knows you and is looking out for you. It's like watching a play and knowing that there is somebody offstage running the show. Here is how some kids put it:

I go out to hear the woods breathe. The only woods in my town are in the park, but if I go there and lie down among the trees, the branches are stirred by the breeze. If I listen really closely, this is like the world breathing. I tell myself, *This is God breathing.*

I talk to God when I am out walking. I say to him, "Nice clouds," or, "You did a good sunrise today." I try to imagine that we are close, that he is listening. And sometimes, you know what? I feel that he is.

CONNECTION

You will begin to connect with the world in a new way. Instead of feeling alone or like a stranger, you will see patterns that include you. The whole creation is connected, and life is nothing but patterns being born and rising to the surface before disappearing like bubbles. Being connected is how you actually are—you are one thread in the cosmic tapestry. It may be a small thread, but all of life would be different without it. Here is how some kids put it:

> I read the stories about great men and women, and when I come across something they did that I can relate to, I feel close to them. My heroes are like me but have gone way beyond me. They lead the way.

> I often stand on an empty beach and stretch out my arms. Then I turn around slowly and say, "This is my home." Since we all came from the sea, it's true that the ocean is my home. Since we all breathe the air, the atmosphere is my home. The light from the sun is part of my home. As I think these thoughts, I feel at home in the whole universe. I belong.

Success

Try to imagine your future. It could go a lot of different ways. What if you wind up getting a very good job, maybe as a doctor or a lawyer, that earns you a lot of money? Imagine yourself with your own house, the beginning of a family, a car you are proud of.

Is this a picture of success?

For most people it is. They see success in material terms, meaning money and status and all the things success can buy. But I think that doesn't really go far enough. Why not have success both outside and inside?

Success is abundance in both the inner and the outer.

It's one thing to be rich in possessions, but another to be rich in love or honor or friendship. Being spiritual doesn't mean you have to give up on the outer riches of life. After all, they are just as much a part of creation as love or beauty. Your soul wants your life to be complete in every way.

In this section we're going to find out how inner and outer abundance can be won. It's clear that teens worry about their future. A sixteen-year-old boy asked:

Dear Deepak,
   Where does motivation come from? I have a hard time

finding any motivation at all, yet other people don't seem to. Is something wrong with me?

This is a major question, because without motivation a person cannot be successful. Everyone has motivation to do certain things. If I ask you to play your favorite video game, eat your favorite food, or talk to your best friend, you will have instant motivation. If someone offers you a lot of money, that becomes a good motivating force also.

MOTIVATION ISN'T IT

But motivation doesn't stick. Tons of people join the gym thinking they are going to get into shape, yet after five or six visits they drop out. You probably have a friend who bought an electric guitar, only to leave it in the corner after a few months or maybe even a few weeks.

Why does motivation wear out? Because it comes from outside yourself.

If you try to motivate yourself from the outside, the day will come when money doesn't work anymore. Buying new stuff stops working also, once you already have more than you need. Being a famous celebrity is basically empty. It's not the real you. Ever.

So to really find your motivation, you can't depend on outside things.

True motivation comes from within. So does true success.

INSPIRATION IS IT

Instead of motivation, look for inspiration. Inspiration comes from the same word as *spirit*. When you are inspired, the spirit moves you. Have you ever seen a sunflower following the sun, turning to follow the sun's path across the sky? A sunflower is fascinating because it never stands still. From sunrise to sunset it turns, naturally seeking the light. The same impulse is everywhere in nature. If you put one-celled animals like amoebas in a dish and shine a light on one side, they will naturally head toward the light also, even though amoebas have no eyes and no nervous system.

That's what inspiration is: the natural tendency to head for the light.

Your soul wants to inspire you.

It wants to show you where your inner light shines.

Going into the Light

Q: I have never seen my inner light. Where is it?

A: Some people actually see a light inside themselves—you'd be surprised how many have seen it at least once. But when you see a picture in your head, that's a form of inner light. The ability to see images is called imagination, and everyone is born with it. Sometimes we say, "You're just imagining things," which makes it sound like the mind's images are a fantasy. But haven't you heard of someone following their dream? That's also imagination, because a dream is just another kind of image.

You need to have a dream you can follow.

When you have your special dream, you will be going into the light.

Special Dreaming

Q: I have dreams at night, but I don't have a special dream. How do I get one?

A: A special dream doesn't come when you are asleep, although it can. Sometimes we know more in our dreams than we think. Some years ago I heard an amazing story about an island in the South Pacific where everyone dreams together. The whole tribe gets up every morning to discuss their dreams,

HOW TO GO INTO THE LIGHT

When you first wake up and are just getting ready for your day, take a few moments to yourself.

STEP 1

Sit quietly until you feel calm and centered. If you have never centered yourself, it's very simple: Just close your eyes and focus your attention where your heart is, right in the center of your chest. Feel your body from this center place and let your mind grow easy and quiet.

STEP 2

Once you are centered, begin to see the day ahead. See yourself as you eat breakfast, go to school, attend class. Be specific and visualize your day *as you would like it to be*. See yourself as

Happy

Confident

Feeling joy and laughter

Meeting no obstacles

Having positive interactions everywhere you go

and whatever the group has dreamed will happen that day, that dream turns into their reality. Basically they dream the future one day at a time.

This made me think that anyone could do the same thing. I began my own special dreaming, but I don't do it when I am asleep.

In fact, the more awake you are, the stronger your dreams will be. They have a better chance of coming true.

The sidebar "How to Go into the Light" shows how it works.

The process of special dreaming starts to work better the more you use it. At first you may find that not every situation comes out exactly the way you wanted. But you will see improvements. Look for them. Believe in them. Here's how one person did it.

STEP 3

If there is any image that makes you feel stressed or anxious when you see it in your mind's eye, pause and stay with that image. Does your body feel tight? Did you stop breathing for a moment? Just relax your body and start to take deep, slow breaths. Do this until the image feels less stressful. See yourself getting through the tough moments very easily and comfortably.

STEP 4

Once you feel easy in your body, say to yourself, "I am writing the future today. It is my future to see and create. I will go forward today as the true author of my life."

Open your eyes and have a great day.

A GOLFER'S TALE

I got really excited about golf a few years ago. I went out for the school team, and the coach said I had some talent. I enjoyed every practice session, yet there were problems. I got very nervous during competition, and sometimes a bad shot made me so frustrated and mad that it would ruin my whole round.

Then I learned to see every hole in advance. I would sit quietly and visualize myself making the perfect tee shot. I could feel how great that would be. I felt the swing going like liquid through my body as the ball soared in a perfect arc and landed in a perfect spot on the fairway.

I would do the same thing for every shot, all the way up to the perfect putt. And it worked. I didn't always make the perfect swing, but I felt much more relaxed. The big change is that now I am playing the game, where before the game was playing me.

That last phrase is really key. You want to feel that you are playing the game of life, not that it is playing you. With special dreaming you can start to put yourself in control of the game, not by forcing things to happen, but by seeing the best outcome for your day and then relaxing and letting things unfold the way they will.

This principle of creating your own reality is very ancient. Thousands of years ago in India the great sages would rise before dawn to do their yoga meditation. They lined their souls up with the energy of the new day, and it was believed that this was enough to bring peace and harmony to everyone in society. I think we need to try that experiment again, so when you do your own special dreaming, congratulate yourself: You are adding to peace and harmony around you every time you go into the light.

Making a Habit of Success

Q: **Do you think successful people have something in common? A certain way of doing things the rest of us don't know?**

A: There's lots of good advice out there about the kind of habits that make someone a success. A lot of that advice centers on how to use your time and how to treat employees and the work staff. That's not really important for teens. You don't have employees, you aren't supporting a family, and your day is managed for you (so far as time goes) when you are at school.

So I sat down and asked myself what I see in the successful people I know, going more toward the spiritual side. I wanted to know more about finding inner fulfillment and growth.

Here's the list of habits I came up with.

Habits for Success:
Dos and Don'ts in Everyday Life

Do follow your inner guide, even if it goes against the group.
Don't be swayed by outside opinion.

Do what feels comfortable and right.
Don't struggle and strain.

Do value who you are. Enjoy your uniqueness.
Don't compare yourself with others and put yourself down.

Do give freely of your time and energy. Make a difference to others
on their journey.
Don't be selfish and act as if only what you want is important.

Do listen to what others say.
Don't be self-centered in your opinions.

Do show respect, even if you disagree with someone else.
Don't assume that only you know what's best.

Do take responsibility for your life.
Don't wait for others to do things for you.

Do have a dream and heroes you look up to.
Don't drift and isolate yourself.

Do keep an open, creative mind, looking for things that are beautiful,
novel, and worth exploring.
Don't stick to your old way of doing and seeing things.

Do trust in the future, which is full of infinite possibilities.
Don't fall prey to short-term setbacks.

Putting this list into play is easy because you can start one point at a time. Each habit for success is within your reach today. Below is a program you might want to follow, although you should feel free to adapt it to your own situation.

A Week of Success: Putting Your New Habits to Work

Day 1

Today is about *being true* to myself. I will look at one situation in my life today where I have been too influenced by peer pressure.

Examples

Defend someone who is unpopular, or speak up for something you believe in, or voice an unpopular opinion that you know is right. If you catch yourself going along with the group just so nobody will criticize you, turn inside to be more true to yourself. Know who you are and what your mind is before following anybody.

Day 2

Today is *Bust the Stress* Day. I will find one thing today that puts stress and strain in my life and try to improve it.

Examples

Make peace with your little brother or sister over some annoying habit. Sincerely tell your parents that they are pressuring you too much in a certain area, like school or homework. At the same time ask them to plan a better way that gets the job done without making you feel so stressed. Look at your schedule and try to get the important tasks done early, so that you are not struggling against a deadline at the last minute. Think about how to use time better in general. Successful people find time precious, so they fill it up with the most important things. Empty time is not a friend.

Day 3

Today is about my *uniqueness*. I will look today for all the things that nobody has in the world but me. I will catch myself if I start putting myself down. I will catch myself when I am tempted to compare myself with somebody I think is better than me. I will find my own special talent and work to make it even better.

Examples

Take your mom and dad aside and say that you want to talk about what makes them feel special. Ask them to say what is special about you, and in return share what you think is special about them. Since you are part of a much bigger picture, sit down and write about the things that make your family special, your school special, your community and nation special. These are also part of your unique place in time and space.

Day 4

Today is about *giving*. I will give of my time and energy today where I know it will be appreciated.

Examples

Without being asked, wash the dishes that have piled up in the sink. Or help your little brother or sister with homework. Or find someone in class who needs help and gently ask if you can assist them. Opportunities to give are everywhere. All you have to do is look for them.

Day 5

Today is about *listening.* I will take special care today to let others express themselves. I will ask for their opinion first, before giving mine. I will catch myself being bored just because I am not the center of attention.

Examples

Pick two topics to bring up at the dinner table, and make sure that everyone in the family knows that they will be able to speak. Ask your mom and dad to tell you more about the work they do. In between classes walk with a favorite teacher and ask why he or she took up teaching as a profession.

Day 6

Today is about *respect.* I will make it clear today that others can open up to me. I will seek a situation where I haven't shown respect and try to correct that.

Examples

At lunch bring up a topic for discussion and say that you want everyone to argue a position opposite of what they usually defend. Find someone who always disagrees with you (generally it's a family member, since they know us the best) and apologize for being so contrary. Afterward ask to hear what they really think.

Day 7

Today is about *responsibility.* I will be as self-reliant today as possible. I will try to pick up the slack where it's needed. I will not just think, *It's not my job.*

Examples

Make your own breakfast or pack your own lunch without being asked. Make breakfast and pack a lunch for your little brother or sister. Do a load of laundry. Vacuum the living room. Make yourself responsible for being where you need to be on time. When you catch yourself whining that you want somebody else to do for you, do for yourself. If you want money, find a way to earn it yourself.

Day 8

Today is about *idealism*. I will take time today to learn more about the life of my heroes and role models. If I know them, I will go talk to them. If they are heroes in history or myth, I will read about their lives and try to apply their ideals to my life.

Examples

Go to a minister or preacher and ask if you could spend some time with him (or her) as he does good works. Visit a disabled person and ask her (or him) where she gets her courage from. Read biographies of great men and women. Look into world mythology to find out what the greatest human adventures have been. In each case apply the story or myth to yourself—become idealistic by absorbing a bit of the great ideals from the past.

Day 9

Today is about *creativity* and opening my mind. I will do one thing today that brings a bit more beauty into the world. I will apply myself today to finding the solution to a problem that faces me.

Examples

Surprise yourself by doing something you'd never dream of doing. If you're the captain of the football team, pick a flower for your English teacher. If you stand around at parties with the same old people, ask somebody to dance. Find a drab little place in your house and make it look nicer: flowers, a bright cloth, a painting, a small piece of art you buy at a secondhand shop. Pick a problem facing humanity that interests you, such as pollution, over-population, AIDS, or poverty. Put yourself in charge of the world and make a list—a blue-sky dreamer's list—of all the ways you would solve such a massive problem. Be as imaginative as you want, without rules or restrictions.

Day 10

Today is about *the future*. I will take time today to think about the future possibilities in my life. I will be positive and imaginative, trying to see myself in many roles doing many things. Wherever I see future problems, I will not lament them, but try to see the best way they can be solved.

Examples

Go to the library and ask for a book about occupations. Spend time learning how someone becomes a doctor or lawyer or small-business owner. Pay attention to the kind of person who really enjoys each kind of work. If you can, actually visit such people. Get a feeling for what life might be like five years or a decade from now. Apply what you learn to yourself. See yourself in as many roles as you are fascinated by. Let your future be as rich and open as possible in terms of personal fulfillment.

SUCCESS PROFILE

As you follow this ten-day program, please don't stop after the first ten days. Keep going through the cycle, not as if it is a chore or a job, but as a way to really take charge of your own success. These success habits are the same ones exhibited by the greatest souls who have ever lived, as well as by wonderful people whose lives are never made famous.

To mark your progress, every ten days return to the following profile. That way you will always be reminding yourself that positive change is happening.

My Growth to Success

Directions: Score 1 to 5 for each statement.
1 = Least improvement
5 = Most improvement

1 2 3 4 5   I am my own person. I don't get that swayed by peer pressure.

1 2 3 4 5   I don't feel pressure as much as before. I am less stressed and worried.

1 2 3 4 5   I'm not comparing myself with others as much. My own talents are emerging.

1 2 3 4 5   I'm more giving to others. I am less selfish.

1 2 3 4 5   I'm a better listener. I pay attention to what other people say and am interested in them.

1 2 3 4 5   I'm not so bothered when someone disagrees with me. I'm starting to appreciate differences.

1 2 3 4 5   I'm more self-reliant. I don't let others take responsibility as much for what is really my responsibility.

1 2 3 4 5   I am a stronger believer in ideals. I am inspired by the lives of others and want my own life to be inspiring.

1 2 3 4 5   I enjoy my creative side more. I'm surprising myself with new ideas and perceptions I didn't have before.

1 2 3 4 5   I feel optimistic about my future. There's a lot more possibility in it than I thought before.

A Success Story

Q: I don't think teenagers are given a real chance to succeed. We are told to be like our parents, which means listening to how they think everything should be done. Is this fair?

A: I sympathize with what you're saying. Until you are old enough to be on your own, there will be conflicts between you and your parents about the right way to do things. This conflict isn't negative as long as you get to win some of the time and they get to win some of the time. In fact, it's very useful to test your ideas about life against theirs. When you finally do go out into the world, you will be yourself, but you will have been partly molded by your parents. Nurturing and freedom go together.

I want to tell you a fantastic story of a teenager who became a multimillionaire. He did it all on his own, and yet he also did it for his family.

SALEEM AND THE COFFEE

Saleem was born to an Indian family who had traveled across the Arabian Sea into Africa. But they didn't get there in an ordinary way. His grandfather ran away from home at the age of eleven, along with his twelve-year-old brother. When they landed in Kenya, they walked all by themselves across the country until they reached the next country of Uganda. They were farm boys, and the long trek was in search of land they could farm.

In Uganda the older brother fell sick and died. Saleem's grandfather started a farm on that spot, planting coffee beans. Young though he was, the farm prospered, and soon there were many workers and a rich harvest that was sold to countries in Europe. By the time Saleem came along, the coffee business was so prosperous that he dreamed as a teenager of becoming a doctor.

But Saleem's father came from the old school of discipline and hard work, and Saleem was sent out into the fields to toil alongside the paid workers. He did as he was told, and soon he got to go to London to sell that year's crop. His father sent the chief foreman along to conduct the transaction, but when they got to England, Saleem found that the buyer had too much coffee already. He offered £2,000 (about $3,200) for each shipload of coffee. Saleem was discouraged and didn't know if he should sell his father's whole crop at such a low price.

Then a remarkable coincidence happened. He went down to the hotel lobby to have tea, and he saw a young woman who looked so sad she was almost crying. Saleem took pity on her and asked what was wrong.

"I have the worst boss in the world," she complained tearfully. "He mistreats everybody, especially me."

"What does your boss do?" asked Saleem.

"He buys coffee," she said. "And he pretends that there is a surplus when the truth is that he is very short of supplies and desperately needs to buy more shiploads. Otherwise he may be ruined."

Saleem couldn't believe his ears. The very man that had made such a stingy offer was this girl's boss. He said nothing to her and went back up to his room. On the next phone call to the buyer Saleem told him that he could have the crop only for the highest going price. Her boss sounded very angry, but in the end he gave in. Saleem had saved his father's business.

This is astonishing enough for a sixteen-year-old boy, but the story takes a mysterious twist. Saleem was afraid for the future in Africa. He saw that a new regime might seize all his father's land and ruin him overnight. So he ordered the foreman to take all the extra money—more than $2 million—and put it in a London bank. They went home and told his father that they had received the usual price for the coffee, which made him happy. Saleem's father had no idea that in secret his son was investing the extra money in banking.

Saleem was so alert and ingenious that he started the first

currency exchange shops in airports, making it easier for tourists to get their money turned back and forth from dollars into local currency. (This was thirty years ago, when exchanging money often took hours in line and a lot of paperwork.) The day came when the boy's prediction came true. A brutal regime took power in Uganda, and overnight his father's whole fortune was seized, along with his land. The father escaped to London with barely $50 in his pocket.

Yet when he landed, there was a limousine waiting at the airport for him. It took him to a fancy hotel, where Saleem, still barely out of his teens, met him with these words:

"I knew this day would come. I have a surprise for you, Father. I took the money we made on that first shipment of coffee, and now I have turned it into ten million dollars. It is all here in the bank waiting for you."

Saleem thought his father would be overjoyed. Instead his father's face turned red and he shouted, "You had no right to lie to me! I am ashamed of you!"

Saleem was usually gentle, but at that moment he got into a furious argument with his father, which ended with his stalking out of the room. The two didn't speak for more than three months.

"I was crushed," Saleem recalls today, "because I had earned all that money for him. But my father was very strict, and to him this was a breach of honor."

After a while Saleem realized that his father knew he'd been rash. Instead of remaining angry, Saleem offered his father forgiveness, and there was a reconciliation. Saleem's father grew very proud of his son's amazing success, and the bond between them became even stronger. This is such a wonderful story because it's not just about material success.

It's about the incredible possibilities that the soul opens up.

It's about fatherly love and a son's love in return.

It's about forgiveness.

It's about realizing that life has to be rich on both the inner and the outer plane to achieve true success.

Fear of Failure

Q: **I am really afraid of failing, so I don't try many new things. How can I change this?**

A: No one loves failure, but if you are too afraid of it, you can't really go out into the world and succeed. Also, when you are feeling self-conscious, as many teenagers do, the bogeyman of failure gets much scarier. It seems as if being young makes each small wound feel so much bigger. Instead of being theoretical about failure, I'll share a telling story someone once told me.

NO FUN DANCING

When I was thirteen, my parents forced me to go to dance class. I kicked and screamed, but they insisted. So I found myself one summer night on the gym floor holding a girl I didn't even know, while a teacher tried to teach us to fox-trot and waltz. I felt very clumsy and stupid.

The teacher must have noticed, because he came over and pulled me and my partner to the front of the class. What a horrible moment! I felt my cheeks grow red; my heart pounded. The teacher made us repeat the same steps over and over, but the more I tried, the clumsier I got. Of course I stepped on the girl's feet, and that wasn't great either.

My torture ended when the teacher

gave up. He shot me a sad smile and said, "Well, I'm sure you'll get better soon." After that nothing could make me go back, and I have avoided social dancing like the plague ever since.

In this tale we find most of the ingredients that make failure so frightening:

Feeling that you will fail in advance

Having your worst beliefs come true

Being seen by others

Suffering humiliation

Running away and never trying again

If you want to overcome your fear of failure, the best way is to tackle each of these ingredients one at a time. Failure is one of those problems that is best solved by breaking it down, instead of trying to charge at it all at once.

FAILING IN ADVANCE

Everyone has a little voice inside that crops up at the worst possible moment to whisper, "You're no good. You'll never do it right. You're bound to fail." Even the most successful people suffer from this little demon inside. Some great actors and singers report that they are almost paralyzed with stage fright before the performance. This happens each and every time, yet they still manage to go on and do wonderful work. So can you.

Some people just tough it out. They believe in the adage "Feel the fear and do it anyway." Maybe your dad thinks you should be that way too, or some coach at school. I am not much of a believer in this approach. If a little kid gets scared in the deep end of the pool and has to be pulled out, you don't want to put him in the deep end again. You start in the shallow end and go easily, one step at a time. That's what we will do here also.

SOME HELPFUL TIPS

Here are some tips on making that little voice of failure go away:

Take deep breaths. Do this steadily and easily for five minutes with your eyes closed.

Visualize a pleasant scene, such as seeing yourself on the beach with palm trees swaying overhead. Feel how wonderful it is to just lie there without a care in the world.

Relax your body—don't pace restlessly.

Be quiet—don't chatter about how nervous you are or hang around people who act nervous and restless. If you have to go off by yourself to calm down, do it. Don't even hesitate.

Stretch your muscles. Most mental tension actually starts in the body and can be released there. A few minutes of simple bending and stretching are all that is needed. Don't exercise to the point of exhaustion, which would be counterproductive to meeting the challenge of what you really want to succeed at.

You can do these things any time you feel the jitters, whether it's before a music performance or a test at school, or before a job interview. They will help.

However, fear of failure can go deeper. You can have more-troubling thoughts, such as

I'll never be any good at this.

Everyone else knows I suck.

If I fail in front of my friends, I'll just die.

What does it matter anyway? It's stupid to win.

Nobody thinks I can succeed, so why should I?

If you have such thoughts, I again want to reassure you that you are not alone. The mind is a funny thing. It uses fear in order to help you. I know that's a peculiar idea, but think about early humans walking the jungle with nothing more than a spear and some rocks. In that primitive state failure to obey your fear could mean death. Everyone had to be alert to danger, which was very real and very physical.

Part of your brain—sometimes called the old brain or the reptilian brain because it developed so long ago in our evolution—still thinks that way. It doesn't know the difference between a small humiliation at dance class and being attacked by a saber-toothed tiger. In both cases powerful hormones are released to provide some "helpful" fear so that you can save your life. In a very real way when you think, *I'm just going to die if that girl turns me down,* part of your brain is being serious.

DEALING WITH FEAR

Fortunately, the old brain isn't the whole story. You have to live with it, but you don't have to let it rule your life. Not by any means. When you are feeling really afraid of failure, do the following three things:

1. *Get a reality check:* Don't just trust your own worst fears. Go talk to someone who cares about you and ask, "How am I doing?" Discuss what you are afraid of. Get a genuine appraisal of how good you really are. Let them reassure you. Try to see yourself through the eyes of someone you really trust.

2. *Restore balance:* Fear can throw you off balance and make you see the world as much scarier than it really is. Realize this: You are young. The weight of the world is not on your shoulders. The future is not your responsibility. You are here to grow naturally, and that doesn't include being scared. Do something you really enjoy when the pressure gets to be too much. Allow time for laughter. Schedule time for things you know you are good at.

3. *Seek improvement:* It's amazing how many people think they are bad at something, when in fact they never learned it properly. You aren't expected to be perfect, or even pretty good, until you put in the time to train. This goes for sports, music, drama, subjects at school, and relationships. Every part of life is a challenge, and we help one another through these challenges by learning, teaching, and sharing. Don't put pressure on yourself beyond your ability. Seek someone who can help you improve. This is a very powerful way to gain confidence, and confidence is the sworn enemy of failure.

If you want to see how things are going, here's a quiz called "A Recipe for Failure." This is the kind of quiz where it's good to get the *lowest score* possible.

A Recipe for Failure: How Many Ingredients Are in Your Cupboard?

Directions:

First, think of a challenge you are afraid to face. It could be making a sports team, passing a test, mastering a skill, or relating to people.

Check any sentence that describes the thoughts or feelings you find yourself having.

☐   This is never going to work. I'm sunk.

☐   Why did I ever want to do this in the first place?

☐   What made me think I could succeed?

☐   This is so unfair. Everything's stacked up against me.

☐   This is too scary. I'm not going to think about it anymore. I'd rather play a video game.

☐   If my friends see me fail, I'm dead.

☐   Everyone else is better than I am. I suck at this.

☐   I tried once before and it didn't work. Why should this time be any different?

☐   I'm just too unlucky.

☐   There's too much stress to put up with.

☐   I don't really fit in.

☐ Other people don't want me around. I'm better off by myself.

☐ I'll just put it off one more day. Things can wait.

☐ It's not like anybody is making me do this.

☐ It's not like anybody is cheering me on.

☐ I'm not really failing. I'm just choosing not to be involved.

☐ Total score

RATINGS
0–3 points

Either you have no fear of failure at all, or you are fooling yourself. To find out which, look at the list "Habits for Success" on page 49 and make sure you are following them.

4–11 points

Things feel pretty scary to you right now. You are thinking a lot about failure and not enough about success. You will benefit quickly from adopting habits for success.

12–16 points

You are paralyzing yourself by seeing the worst. Things are better than you think. You should start today to develop more habits for success.

How to Be Exceptional

Q: I would like to have a really exceptional life. Is there one secret to doing that?

A: An exceptional life is one that reaches for the highest possibilities. I do think there is a secret to this. The secret can be named in one word: *Vision.*

Many people don't know this secret. They don't realize that spirit helps us reach our visions, but first the vision has to exist. Give someone a vision of happiness, a vision of a better future, a vision of a loving family, or a vision of the ideal life, and suddenly there are invisible forces that will come to help make that vision a reality.

TELL ME YOUR VISION

This also goes back to motivation. When someone asks, "How can I get motivated?" I immediately say, "First tell me your vision." If they don't have one, right away we both know why they aren't feeling motivated. I'm going to simplify things, but here are sketches of two people, one who has a vision and one who doesn't.

The *visionary* lives with a goal and a purpose. If you ask, "What is your life about?" such a person has an answer. Every day brings him (or her) closer to his vision. He can see the future before him. Images come to mind; he feels his vision getting more and more real. There are discouraging days when he has to take a step backward, or maybe more than one step, but soon his vision is ignited again, and like a fire in the heart, it drives him forward.

Examples would be great artists like Pablo Picasso and Michelangelo, great political leaders like Mahatma Gandhi and Abraham Lincoln, great souls like Mother Teresa and Nelson Mandela.

The *nonvisionary* is adrift. Such a person follows the crowd. She (or he) likes what most people like, she does what most people do. She is happy when things go her way, but if they don't, she feels really miserable. The future seems uncertain or perhaps worse—it could be empty. A nonvisionary has to go with the crowd because if she struck out on her own, she would be like a ship lost at sea. It's much easier to live a safe life with small expectations.

I don't have to name examples because society contains millions of nonvisionaries. But you don't have to be famous to have a vision. Everyone should have one. All it takes is a desire to have spirit be on your side. Spirit is the home of visions, because at the level of the soul anything is possible.

FOUR KEY QUESTIONS

For someone like you, a person young enough to make almost any choice in life, this is a great time to choose your own vision. You don't have to accept anyone else's. You can model your future—or at least the next few years—according to your own viewpoint.

To have your own vision means asking four questions:

What kind of person do I want to be?

What kind of work is best for me?

What kind of life do I see myself leading?

What is my deepest desire and highest hope?

Every exceptional life came about by asking these questions. There's no such thing as becoming exceptional by accident, or by sitting back and letting it come to you. Recently I read a story about a fifteen-year-old girl in Denver who did something exceptional. She started a political movement all on her own. The movement centered on one issue: cruelty to animals. This girl began to feel that it was cruel for circuses to travel around with animals in cages. The more she thought about it, the more she felt that it was unnatural for animals to be confined behind bars and let out only to do tricks for people.

She could have forgotten the whole idea and done nothing. She could have printed up a few leaflets and passed them out at the circus the next time it came to town. Instead she did something exceptional. She managed to collect enough signatures to get the issue on the ballot so that Denver voters could decide for themselves. It's thought that she is the youngest person ever to have put an issue on a ballot, but now the voters will be able to choose whether the circus can come to Denver or not.

MAKING IT PERSONAL

You can see how this girl was acting on a vision, and although I haven't talked to her personally, I can imagine how she would answer our four questions:

What kind of person do I want to be?
A person who cares.

What kind of work is best for me?
Political activism within my community.

What kind of life do I see myself leading?
The life of a leader or activist.

What is my deepest desire and highest hope?
To see a world without cruelty to any living creature.

If you can answer the same four questions yourself, you can find your own vision and put it into action. (I don't necessarily mean political or community action, but the action that feels right for you.) None of these are trick questions, but they are really hard to answer anyway. What makes them hard is that teens (and many adults) only want to be what looks good in someone else's eyes.

BE YOURSELF

Pressure from your peers and family makes it hard to have your own vision and not just a copy of somebody else's. You know, in all the questions I received for this book, not a single teenager asked me how to find their own vision. So I know there's a lot of work to do in this area. I did get a lot of questions that wanted to know about being rich or famous or a celebrity—which tells me that young people are too often addicted to the empty, shiny promises of Madison Avenue. Yet if you live according to your own vision, you will have the kind of fulfillment that most celebrities can only dream about. You will most probably wind up happier than the rich, believe it or not.

So how are you going to answer those four questions?

A good idea would be to ask your soul to answer for you. If your soul could do that—and remember, your soul is a part of you, not a strange alien living in outer space or on a cloud—its answers would be something like this:

What kind of person do I want to be?
A person of peace and love who experiences joy.

What kind of work is best for me?
The kind that satisfies me deeply.

What kind of life do I see myself leading?
A life of freedom, where every day is a new world.

What is my deepest desire and highest hope?
To find out the truth about myself.

Now we're getting close to a real vision. It isn't yet your vision. It doesn't have your name on it, your own personal touch. We're going to add the personal touch in the next chapter, which is about finding the good life. What's the good life going to be for you? Well, I haven't met you, but there's one thing that has to be present for any life to be good. Love and health are contained in it. So are satisfaction and a spiritual fire in the heart. What is this one thing we all must have?

I simply call it well-being.

Well-Being

"HOW DO I FIND TRUE HAPPINESS?"

I'm sure you want a good life. Everyone does. But not everyone winds up having a good life. What's the secret? Teenagers worry about this a lot, often more than their parents guess. Here are two letters from opposite sides, but somehow they meet in the middle. The first is from a sixteen-year-old girl.

> **Dear Deepak,**
>   **When am I going to be happy? I feel so blah most of the time. Is this how I'm supposed to feel when I am so young?**

The second came from an eighteen-year-old boy.

> **Dear Deepak,**
>   **I am going to graduate this year, and I guess this sounds crazy, but what if high school turns out to be the best time of my life? How can I tell if everything is down-hill from here?**

The first person is worried that she will never be happy because she isn't happy now. The second person is happy now but is worried that it won't last. There's an old saying that happiness is fleeting. I don't think that has to be, and neither does your soul.

Well-being is a permanent part of you.

This is where the two questions meet in the middle. Both teens want to know how to make happiness last. And my answer to both is that happiness lasts only if it comes from inside you, and the deeper the well of happiness, the more intense it will be all your life.

FINDING THE OPPORTUNITY

I don't want to shock anyone who feels blah or depressed or miserable, but really you have an opportunity in disguise here. You have an incentive to make your own happiness, because you have experienced how sorrowful it is to do without. And being a young person, you are just the right age to learn how to create well-being for yourself. Many adults are stuck in ruts that have been worn down for many years. They know more than you do about life, but they have less ability to create something new. So congratulate yourself, even if you don't feel wonderful today.

I am calling this chapter *Well-Being* instead of *Happiness* because well-being includes more things. Happiness can be just a mood that will change when things go wrong. Well-being is stronger and more permanent. When you have it, you feel comfortable in your body. You appreciate nature and the beauty around you. You feel love. You value other people. You have a sense of inner security that is hard to shake. Put these all together and I think the thing that everyone wants—a good life—is very reachable.

First, however, let's look at your sense of well-being right now.

A Happiness Quiz

Directions:

Read each sentence and respond by checking *Yes* or *No*. Give yourself 1 point for every *Yes* answer.

☐ Yes ☐ No   I like my body.

☐ Yes ☒ No   I get enough sleep and exercise.

☐ Yes ☐ No   I have good, happy thoughts about myself.

☐ Yes ☐ No   I rarely get depressed or down.

☐ Yes ☐ No   I find it pretty easy to stay out of trouble.

☐ Yes ☐ No   I don't drink or take drugs.

☐ Yes ☐ No   I have true friends who stand by me.

☐ Yes ☐ No   I can share pretty much anything with my friends.

☐ Yes ☐ No   I don't fall into being hard on myself.

☐ Yes ☐ No   Others treat me like one of the good guys, which I am.

☐ Yes ☐ No   I have a spiritual life that comforts me and helps me grow.

☐ Yes ☐ No   I believe in a personal God.

☐ Yes ☐ No   I spend some time every week doing good for others.

☐ Yes ☐ No   It makes me feel good to give.

☐ Yes ☐ No   I am good about my temper. I don't get into big fights or arguments.

☐ Yes ☐ No   I say what I feel. I don't store up resentments or grudges.

☐ Yes ☐ No   I love being outdoors. I make time for nature.

☐ Yes ☐ No   I would rather see a beautiful sunset than play a video game or watch TV.

☐ Yes ☐ No   Every year my life is getting better.

☐ Yes ☐ No   I am optimistic about my future.

☐ Total score

RATINGS
0-6 points

Unhappiness is a big issue for you. You don't feel that you have anyone you can share your real feelings with. Yet despite how alone you often feel, you can make a good life for yourself. The key is to turn yourself around by following a new path that will show you how to feel better about yourself. There's a lot of hope for you once you are given the right keys.

7-14 points

Most of the time you are happy, but in your down moments you have quite a few doubts. By working on your own well-being, you can make a lot of progress. Now is the best time of your life to discover the secrets of happiness and truly apply them.

15–20 points

You have a very good sense of well-being that has developed from an early age. Now it's up to you to share your happiness. If you look, you will find plenty of others who would benefit from the light that comes so naturally to you.

THE REAL YOU IS HAPPY

Happiness feels easy and simple if you are happy already. It's much more complicated when you're not. But the good news is this: *Well-being is the real you.* Your soul contains a deep reservoir of well-being that you can tap into. When you find the real you, you will be secure, at peace, and joyful in your heart. This is true at any age, old or young. It is the spiritual promise we were all born to fulfill.

Why haven't you found the real you already?

Because your life has gotten too complicated. Because it's easier to coast through, even when you don't feel so great. Because no one gave you any helpful information about making your own happiness. For all these reasons and more, teens often wind up feeling miserable without seeing a way out.

To be honest, these can be the toughest years of life emotionally. But take heart: These are also years of great promise and incredible potential.

Whether you feel great at this moment or not, there is a way to create well-being for yourself. First I will outline the program, then we will take each point one at a time.

TEN KEYS TO WELL-BEING:
Daily Promises to Keep

1. I will make sure my body is healthy.

2. I will make sure my mind is healthy.

3. I will do what I know is right.

4. I will be around people who really care for me.

5. I won't judge against myself or put myself down.

6. I will make friends with spirit.

7. I will make a contribution.

8. I will avoid violence in all its disguises.

9. I will cherish nature.

10. I will never stop growing.

If you can keep these promises to yourself, you will be doing the maximum to create well-being in your life. This list is a life plan that works on all levels, starting with your body but also including mind, relationships, self-image, and emotions.

Want to know the secret of happiness?

The secret of happiness is to include all these levels. Each one counts.

A BALANCED LIFE

Now you know the secret, so you can stop struggling to make yourself happier or pretending to be happy when you're really not. All you have to do is include all of yourself in a balanced approach to life. It's the most natural way and the one that works the best.

You'd be amazed how many people neglect one or more of these levels. The champion athlete has a body to die for, but he may forget how to relate to others or how to have a strong self-image when he loses a game. The genius in math class may forget that he has a body or that there is a beautiful world of nature to explore. The girl with the totally charming personality may turn her back on giving happiness to others rather than just taking all the time. These imbalances are not good for lasting well-being.

I want each point in the program to sink in personally, so each one will include three personal profiles. Mark the profile that *best applies to you right now*. In this way you will have a good starting point for seeing how much progress you make as you continue on your spiritual journey.

Profile #1 is a person with a *strong sense of well-being.*

Profile #2 is a person with an *average sense of well-being.*

Profile #3 is a person with a *fair to poor sense of well-being.*

I don't imagine you will see yourself exactly in any single

profile—you don't have to—but they outline some typical beliefs that I've encountered over the years among many young people.

THE FIRST KEY TO HAPPINESS:
A Healthy Body

Which profile is closest to you?

Profile #1

I like my body. I exercise more than most kids because it feels good. I don't obsess over my physical looks. I realize that my body is my friend and support system. I respect that and don't put things into my body that aren't good for it.

Profile #2

My body is just there. I don't notice it unless I get sick or there's a situation that makes me feel self-conscious. Exercise isn't my thing—I prefer to hang out in my room doing other stuff. I'm pretty hooked on junk food. I may or may not have used drugs and alcohol.

Profile #3

I feel bad saying this, but sometimes I just hate my body. Why isn't it as good as other people's? I worry about how others see me. I know they think I am not good enough physically. Body issues are major with me, and yet as much as I want a better body, I do abuse it with the wrong food or too much food. My impulse control is awful. Help!

A MEDICAL DISCOVERY

The first key to happiness is a healthy body. Your body makes a big difference in your sense of well-being. One of the big medical discoveries since you were born is the discovery that our bodies help make us happy or unhappy. Certain brain chemicals, such as

serotonin, actually make your mood better. If you can increase these natural mood enhancers, things that once got you down won't be as strong. You may have heard about the runner's high, a natural sense of euphoria that many people feel when they exercise. That's a good example of how a purely physical act can increase the chemicals (called endorphins) that help raise your mood.

So being into your body isn't just about looking good. In fact, looking good—in the sense of striving for the perfect body—doesn't necessarily trigger the right chemicals. You can be the most beautiful supermodel and yet feel so insecure that your body will produce exactly the opposite chemicals, the ones that raise your inner stress level. You can be a champion football player and wind up with so many injuries that your life becomes wracked with pain for years afterward.

STRESS DOESN'T HELP

It's not good to force your body into doing what you or somebody else wants. A lot of people forget this. A fifteen-year-old boy asked:

Dear Deepak,
    I come from an athletic family, and when I was younger, my father pushed me into heavy-duty physical activity. I don't really like to train hard, but I'm afraid I will be a wuss if I don't. What can I tell my father that will make him lighten up?

Tell him that doctors have proved over and over that stress is much worse for a person than exercise is good. When you enjoy exercising, your whole body courses with chemicals that alleviate stress, such as serotonin and dopamine, whereas when you hate to exercise, your body is flooded with chemicals that increase stress, such as cortisone and even adrenaline. (Contrary to the popular myth of the adrenaline high, this hormone breaks down tissues and

leads to physical and mental exhaustion if too much is released into the body or if it is released too often.) Nor is it all-important to go in for heavy workouts. It's the right activity, not pushing it to the limit, that gives a sense of well-being. What's the right activity?

GOOD ACTIVITY FOR THE BODY

- A little light exercise that gets you off the couch and away from the computer

- Exercise that makes you feel better after you've finished than you felt before you began

- Any physical activity that relaxes your mind

- An activity that is in balance with the rest of your life

These points are easy to apply once you put your mind to it. One thing that few people know is that it is more important to do any kind of exercise than to keep totally fit. The biggest health risks, such as heart disease and diabetes, face those who do absolutely

nothing but sit at home or work all day in an office. Once you get out for a brisk walk four times a week, you have made the biggest step toward avoiding those risks. Going further and becoming totally fit is also good, but that is more or less icing on the cake.

NO PAIN, NO GAIN?

I am not a great fan of the "No pain, no gain" school of sports. It works for someone who is highly competitive and motivated to win at all costs. That doesn't include 90 percent of teens, which may explain why the number of teens who exercise has fallen off steadily since the early 1960s. Today only about 6 percent of the adult population engages in any regular exercise—the most popular being walking.

So start early, before you get so adjusted to sitting around all day that your only exercise is going to the refrigerator to see if there's still some leftover pizza inside. I know that for many kids PE class was an early torture that gave exercise a bad name. If that's true for you, then don't force yourself to go out for a team sport or any activity that would open you up to mean remarks from other kids. You can bike on your own or with a friend. You can talk for an hour with your buddy while walking, instead of lying on your bed with a phone to your ear.

"I HATE MY BODY"

Let's say that the situation isn't good at all, that you really hate your body. This question from a fifteen-year-old girl comes from such a place:

Dear Deepak,
     Why are kids so mean to someone just because they are fat?

My heart goes out to her because kids can be very cruel. Children today are getting to be overweight at an earlier and earlier age. She has probably endured some hard teasing for quite a long time (which would no doubt make her eat even more in order to numb the pain). Young people in general have become terribly self-conscious about body image.

Here's the advice a teen with a weight problem will usually get:

"You're beautiful in other ways."

"You're such a great person. Forget the weight."

"You are so fortunate in other areas."

"Don't think about yourself so much."

"Your problem is that you don't have enough discipline."

"I don't see you as fat."

"Have another bowl of ice cream. You'll feel better."

None of this is really helpful when kids are being so mean to you that you barely want to show your face in public. Of course there's the sensible advice, which is to go on a diet and stop eating so much. But that can be very hard to do when you're stuck in bad habits, or when your whole family uses food to feel good, or when other things make you feel so sad that eating is about the only thing that makes you forget. Overeating is an emotional problem most of the time, not a purely physical one. And even if it starts out being a physical problem, emotional issues take over once the teasing and the bad self-image start to pile up.

In some societies beauty is measured by how well fed a girl looks, and it is the little skinny girls who don't fit in. But skinny or fat, you're not going to be perfect. You're not always going to fit in. You'll have to live with people who don't care how you feel.

BETTER ADVICE

I would like to offer another kind of advice: *Make a good life for yourself anyway.*

If you work on all ten points of the well-being program, one day you are going to feel so good about yourself that one of two things will happen: (1) You will realize that being overweight is not the tragedy you think it is now; (2) You will feel so good about yourself that the emotional reasons for overeating will disappear. Until one of these two things happens, you will find it very difficult to get rid of the extra weight. It is serving you. As much as you hate the mean kids, you need food more.

I know this sounds funny. Most overweight kids are really miserable inside about how they look. But here's another secret that not enough of us realize: *Pain doesn't motivate people to change.* Whether it is the fat kid who is mercilessly teased, the chain-smoker who can barely breathe and faces all kinds of diseases, or the addict who has caused immense grief to everyone around him or her, pain isn't enough. All these bad habits are terrible for the body. They are terrible for achieving well-being. Yet until something better comes along, these habits are often the only way a person knows to feel good.

MIND-BODY CONNECTIONS

You see, the body is connected to the mind. If you have a rock in your shoe, you can just say, "Ouch," and pull it out. It's a no-brainer. But when the mind enters in, there is psychological pain to deal with. Then things get more complicated than having a rock in your shoe. I meet lots of overweight adults who eat only skimpy salads in public and yet sneak extra pieces of chocolate cake when they are in private. Something psychological makes them do that. It's a war between the "good me" and the "bad me." We all take part in that war. The only way to win it is to make such a good life for yourself that the "good me" is empowered. When it feels strong enough, you will be able to look the "bad me" in the face and start to work on its problems.

That's the deep reason for asking you to be good to your body. You need to get it on the side of the "good me," because you deserve it. Your soul already knows that all of you is good, and as you grow, you will arrive at the same realization.

DRINKING AND DRUGS

Now for the darker side of how teens use their bodies. A junior in high school asked:

> **Dear Deepak,**
> My parents are totally opposed to me drinking or using any kind of recreational drug. That's fine, but they don't realize how common alcohol and drugs are at school. Isn't it better for me to tell them that I use occasionally than to sneak around behind their backs?

It wouldn't be honest for me to say that it's completely wrong to use alcohol and drugs. Adults have been telling their kids to avoid both for decades, and yet at a time when almost every school has antidrug classes, the use of drugs is at or near an all-time high. Peer pressure makes kids try drugs and alcohol. Curiosity and the lure of a guilty pleasure reinforce the peer pressure.

So the real question isn't what you tell your parents—after all, you already know that they are dead set against your using. The real question is what you tell yourself. Morality can only go so far. At a certain point each of us is responsible for our own actions. If a teen is younger, from twelve to fifteen, I would agree with parents who go to almost any length to keep their child clean and sober. I say this not out of alarm that one drink will ruin someone's life, but out of knowing that it's unfair to ask a young teen to make adult decisions when something as volatile as drugs or alcohol is concerned.

From age sixteen on up I think you are old enough to know yourself a bit better. One drink or one pill will tell you if you are going to use sensibly or not. An experiment is useful in telling you more about yourself. Once the curiosity passes, the vast majority of kids will walk away of their own accord.

SOCIAL DRINKING?

However, the big exception is social drinking. Teens now use alcohol far more than previous generations. Alcohol is wrongly considered the "harmless" drug, when in fact it is associated with huge numbers of highway deaths, crime, domestic violence, and accidents. Ask yourself the most basic question: Why drink at all? The answer is that it makes you feel good. Alcohol takes away inhibitions, at least in small doses. But it is also a toxic substance, an obvious fact, given that a single overdose can kill you.

Since antialcohol campaigns have done little to discourage teen drinking—especially binge drinking—I can offer one new idea. If drinking makes you feel free, try to become that free without alcohol. Your soul can make you that free. Alcohol makes you feel good because its molecules fit into certain receptors on the outside of brain cells. Those same receptors can be filled with molecules that you produce yourself. Look at the joy on the face of someone who has just won the lottery or fallen in love, and you are seeing the result of receptor sites being filled spontaneously, without the use of an outside drug. Which brings us to a general rule about substance abuse: *If you are addicted to one kind of pleasure, the best way to end your addiction is to find a greater pleasure.*

HOW ADDICTIONS WORK

Contrary to popular opinion, it's not the drug that makes the addict. A hundred people can take a drink and walk away without feeling addicted, compared with those five or six who cannot. For them the drink leads to addiction for other reasons:

Alcohol makes them feel better than they can on their own.

It gives them a way to forget their troubles.

It gives them a way to forget themselves.

It leads to a temporary sense of power and freedom.

It provides false self-esteem.

If you look at this list, everything on it is good. It's good to have pleasure, self-esteem, a sense of personal power and freedom. These are, in fact, some of the highest personal goals in life. Most people can tell the difference between the real thing, however, and the kind induced by drugs and alcohol. Addicts can't. They want to access these good things but fail without the use of an outside substance. In that sense addiction is a spiritual problem. The best antidote, I believe, is to pursue spirit and try to fill the empty spaces inside yourself. I am not all that concerned about recreational drugs and alcohol; I am more concerned about people who feel empty and soulless. If you can rid yourself of those feelings, then substance abuse disappears automatically.

THE SECOND KEY TO HAPPINESS:
A Healthy Mind

Which profile is closest to you?

Profile #1

I like what goes on in my mind. I have good thoughts about myself and other people. My imagination comes up with things that delight me. I feel mentally fresh, and I like a good challenge to my intellect. I know there will always be someone smarter than me, but I will make the best use of the intelligence I was given.

Profile #2

My mind's okay, but it lets me down sometimes. I can remember being embarrassed in school because I said something dumb in class. I'd rather use my mind to play a video game or figure out sports statistics than to study. Being average mentally is okay, I guess, but I admit that I keep away from mental challenges most of the time.

Profile #3

I don't want to think about my mind. I'm not into that game. I mostly shut up in class. I have bad memories of school, starting pretty early. Nobody has encouraged me to think or use my imagination. Secretly I wonder if maybe I am as dumb as others might suppose.

SMART OR DUMB?

Smart and *dumb* are loaded words, and I try not to use them. Einstein himself was considered dumb in his early youth. Now, as then, people make snap judgments. Many a child with bad eyesight or poor hearing has wound up in remedial classes because some adult didn't take the time to see that the problem wasn't lack of intellect, but a disability. And the mind isn't the same from person to person. Each of us has strong points and weak points in how we use our mind. The average American adult can read and reason fairly well, yet not be able to draw beyond the level of a grade-schooler. (How different in Switzerland, where everyone, not just the artistic kids, learns to draw.) In many schools the shop classes are for the "dumb" kids, and yet in a country like New Zealand the smart kids are in there learning how to do household repairs and work with their hands. When you are old enough to own your own home, you may mourn the day you didn't learn how to fix an overflowing toilet or install a tile floor. The so-called dumb kids get their revenge when they grow up and turn into skilled craftspeople.

The real question is whether your mind adds to the good life. All the very best things come through the mind: Art and science.

Joy and love. Dreams and imagination. But the mind can get discouraged, and when that happens, it stops contributing to the good life. I find that with teens this is the biggest problem, that they have discouraged minds and don't realize it.

Here are some symptoms of a discouraged mind.

A DISCOURAGED MIND:
Do You Fit Any of These Symptoms?

Giving up on lessons in class

Blowing off class, ignoring deadlines for homework

Sitting back in class and not participating

Acting up in class, turning into a clown or a rebel to attract attention

No longer reading for pleasure

Not using your imagination

Keeping your thoughts to yourself

Refusing to debate your beliefs and pet ideas

Becoming narrow and prejudiced in your thinking

The early things on this list are the most obvious. Kids who have given up on school aren't hard to spot. But did you think that the class clown might have a discouraged mind? Or the narrow-minded bigot who says nasty things to people of color? When it's healthy, the mind isn't narrow, and there's no need to clown around or put people down when what you really want is to be proud of your mind.

MAKING IT BETTER

The first step in getting a healthy mind is to heal any signs of discouragement. Do it early, before you go too far and there's not enough time to catch up with your dreams for yourself. If you allow your mind to remain discouraged, you will settle for second best on your dreams or give up altogether. Your mind will get healthier the more you use it in the right way. Here's a list for that, too.

A HEALTHY MIND:
Using Your Mind in the Right Way

Read good things instead of junk.

Use your imagination.

Think for yourself, not the way you've been told to think.

Accept new challenges.

Don't give up so easily. Go back and think again.

Be around people smarter than you. Enjoy and appreciate them, don't worry about competing.

Find a mental hobby (other than video games).

Learn a bit of math and science.

Get into good, hard discussions.

Think about the big picture, such as world peace and AIDS.

Use your mind to help others.

What's important about this list is that everything on it adds to the good life. Your mind is the most important partner in your well-being. It's not about IQ. Share your thoughts with people who care and who listen. The adults I know who have healthy minds aren't always the big brains—they are people who follow the things on this list. You can have a huge intellect, forming pet theories of immense complication, and yet hide yourself away from the world and have very unhealthy mental habits. I also know bright kids who feel very sad and bitter that nobody in their family will talk with them or share ideas. Either the other family members are intimidated—you'd be amazed how many fathers and mothers are intimidated by a bright youngster—or just don't care.

But you have to care. The mind is a muscle like any other, and if you neglect it, it will start to wither away. Of course, in a way this whole book is about having a healthy mind, because spiritual experiences must come through the nervous system also. There's no such thing as a mindless awakening. It takes alertness and willingness and desire, all of which come through your mind. Your mind can be one of the glories of your life.

Look at the profiles in the next section. They describe the kinds of mental attitudes kids often take. You won't fit any of them perfectly, but they might tell you something about yourself.

THE THIRD KEY TO HAPPINESS:
Doing the Right Thing

Which profile is closest to you?

Profile #1

I definitely see myself as one of the good guys. I have stood up for someone in trouble. I've walked away when other kids tried to get me to do something I knew was wrong. I don't judge others. Being good is a private thing, and I know what my values are. I'm open-minded about any lifestyle that doesn't hurt anybody. I devote some time every month to helping those in need.

Profile #2

Sure, I'm good, but I like to do what I want too. If I found a wallet on the street, I'd be tempted to keep at least some of the money inside. I've been known to sneak around if I really want something badly, and I'm not that thrilled with authority. Mostly I have a good conscience, though, as long as I don't look at myself too hard.

Profile #3

Hey, it's good to be bad. I don't think others have a right to tell me how to behave. I'm my own man (or woman). I know what it's like to get into trouble, but I get by. I cut corners when I have to, and I have good enough luck and smarts not to get caught. Sometimes I have a bad conscience, and I know that other kids don't have a good opinion of me, but so what? I'm past the point of no return, or very close to it.

WHY DO WE DO THE WRONG THING?

I just talked about the discouraged mind. When someone goes even further past discouragement, something new happens. They stop doing what they know to be right. Most criminals, as marked by society, know right from wrong. But they long ago lost the ability to figure out how to do what they know is right. They feel that the "bad me" took over somewhere along the line. They might even say that "it," the force of evil, is in control. But these extreme cases began with something simple: not acting on good impulses and giving in to bad ones.

To have a sense of well-being, you need to act on your good impulses. The bad impulses aren't going to vanish. They want to have their say; they are going to compete for your attention. So the issue isn't about being an angel or so goody-goody that you start believing in your own sainthood. The issue is about being alert enough that you can tell good from bad when it counts.

THE MOMENT OF DECISION:
When Does Good and Bad Really Count?

When your actions might injure you or another

When you might humiliate another

When you know you are going to feel guilty tomorrow

When you might hurt an important relationship

When you might open the way for even more bad things

When you might violate someone else's right

When you might give away your dignity

When you might lower yourself in your own eyes

Some parents would be shocked by this list because it doesn't begin with "When you break the law" or "When you disobey your parents." It's not that I don't think those things are important. They are. But laws and parental rules exist outside yourself. Desire exists inside yourself. When it comes to a contest, the external rule is almost always going to lose out. So many teens act on desires for alcohol or sex or cutting school or breaking the law because they want to know how it feels. Rules feel cold. That's just the nature of rules. Desire feels warm, or maybe even burning.

BETTER CHOICES

So at the moment of decision you need to go to other things that are also inside you. If you look at the list again, you will see that each point centers on something desirable about yourself:

Wanting to be a good person

Keeping your dignity and self-esteem

Not wanting to hurt anybody else

Not wanting to feel guilty after it's too late to change things

Wanting to feel safe and in control

There is a lot of emotion attached to bad or reckless desires, but there's emotion attached to these good things also. Only you can find the balance. That's the key to living with both the "good me" and the "bad me." Crossing the line isn't forbidden, but you know when it's okay. Letting loose can be very good for you. Losing your inhibitions will show you a side of yourself you might not ever meet otherwise. No one is asking you to be the preacher's daughter or son (they are often the first to run into temptation that's too sweet to refuse). The point is that doing the right thing is part of the good life. It builds a better self than if you do the wrong thing. It builds a better self than if you shrug your shoulders and decide not to think about good and bad. Good and bad will always be with us, and navigating a true course between them will always be one of life's greatest rewards.

THE FOURTH KEY TO HAPPINESS:
Someone Who Cares

Which profile is closest to you?

Profile #1

My family loves me, and at least one family member is like my best friend. I am not afraid to say how I really feel. They respect me and listen to what I have to say. I know I will always have people in my life who care for me as a person.

Profile #2

I have a good family, but we don't spend a lot of time together. Everyone is off doing their own thing. I'm careful what I say sometimes—it's not always that good if I say what I really think. I wish I had someone I could really confide in, but at least I have pretty good friends, and I expect to be friends with a few of them for a long time.

Profile #3

My family doesn't understand me very well. There are rules and behavior at my house that I don't agree with. But it's not like my opinion counts, so I toe the line at home and save what I really want to do for my own time and my own friends. We have a good time together, but to tell you the truth, I don't share any deep stuff with the friends I hang out with.

BELONGING

One important part of being happy is to feel that you belong. Belonging isn't just about being part of a clique or a gang or even a posse of friends who hang out together. It's about bonding with someone so closely that you can say anything you feel like saying. Being young is an experimental time. You have to try on different ways of talking about yourself, different moods and ideas that just come to you. In a few years these attitudes will probably change a great deal, but you won't know how they feel right now unless you try them out.

I can remember walking down the street in India trying on all kinds of attitudes with my close buddies. We'd pretend to be outlaws or movie stars. We'd act tough one minute, then turn into excited children the next. I think that was a very productive period, and I hope you are going through it too. But one thing I learned only much later: You have to open up to people who care about you. Otherwise you're just pretending to put on attitudes. You are going along to get along.

The deeper someone else cares for you, the deeper you care for yourself.

WHEN SOMEBODY REALLY CARES

This is one of life's spiritual rules, even though lots of teens try to duck out of it. They pretend not to care. They try to go it alone. They keep secrets and develop a private world in their room. Yes, you can retreat into a private world for a while, but it's not a real substitute for hearing someone else say such things as

"You're great. I don't know what I'd do without you."

"I love hearing what you have to say."

"You really know your own mind. I like that."

"People are going to want to listen to you."

It would be great if every teen heard these words at home. Even if you don't, it's up to you to find a way to hear them from somebody. You need a reflection of your worth. That's how real, lasting self-confidence is built. You get to know that you matter. You don't matter *if*. That is, you don't matter *if* you're smart, or *if* you do what your parents say, or *if* you're good-looking and popular. All those *if*s are irrelevant. You should matter just because you are you. Is that an idea you already agree with? Ask yourself the following questions:

Am I sure I'd be forgiven at home if I did something really wrong?

Would my parents sympathize if my grades fell, or would they look disappointed and critical?

If I dated a black person or became best friends with a gay person, would my clique still like me?

If I passed out political buttons at school for an unpopular candidate, would my friends still respect me?

MAKING THE GRADE

In your life these may be hypothetical questions. The real-life situations might never come up. Yet the time always arrives when you'll find out if people care for you just because you're you, or if they want something from you instead. Friends of course have a right to want things. They want companionship. They want us to sympathize with them. They want shared interests and like opinions. If you fall into line and give these things, it's fairly smooth sailing.

One girl said to me, "I hung around with my best friend for four years, and then one day she suddenly turned to me and said, 'Don't come over to my house anymore. We're finished.' I was totally shocked, but after a while I realized that in all those years I'd never had the nerve to ask her how she really felt about me. I guess she had some pretty bad feelings, and the only way she could let them out was to say good-bye. I learned a lesson there. Now

even if I'm a little afraid, I try to find out how someone really feels about me before we get too deep."

Like this girl, you need to know if you are wanted just for yourself. Maybe you'll dare to step out and do something the crowd doesn't like. Then things will get really interesting. There's a lot to be said about this. In the next chapter on relationships, I'll go deeper into how to make true friends. For the moment just know that to really enjoy a sense of well-being, you have to care deeply about yourself and be with people who care for you just as much.

THE FIFTH KEY TO HAPPINESS:
No Self-Judgment

Which profile is closest to you?

Profile #1

I feel pretty complete and happy with myself. I don't get intimidated. Others can't put me down because I don't put myself down. I don't care what others say about me. It may hurt for a day, but I forget their opinion and go on doing what I always do: trying to be the best me I can be.

Profile #2

I have an all right self-image, but I get shaky when the going gets rough. It hurts when other kids are mean, and in secret I wonder if they say other bad things behind my back. Worse, those bad things may be true. But on the whole I am getting by pretty well, and once I am grown up, I expect to feel better about myself.

Profile #3

I've been told that I'm too hard on myself. Yes, I can be self-critical. But I've always been that way, and I'd rather see the bad parts of myself first, before someone hurts my feelings by pointing them out later. I can say things about them that are just as mean as what they can say about me. If I could find a way not to be down on myself so much, I'd love to stop, but no one has ever showed me how.

SELF-DOUBT

A whole book could be written—and I'm sure has been—on why teens are so hard on themselves. Self-doubt seems to be part of the package during these in-between years. But that doesn't mean that it is natural to judge against yourself. A lot of things are new. You are experiencing them for the first time, and therefore doubt can be a healthy thing. It helps to show you whether you are going to be good at something like baseball or math or dancing or being in a rock band. Unhealthy doubt isn't helpful because it says, "You're not going to be any good at this," before you even start.

DOUBT CAN BE HEALTHY

This is such an important issue that I want to expand on it. Think of something you were really in doubt about. It could be anything where the outcome was uncertain, maybe in the dating scene or going out for sports or trying a new activity. Which kind of thoughts went through your head?

Two Kinds of Doubt

Healthy doubt says, "Maybe I'll be good at this, maybe not."
Unhealthy doubt says, "I'm going to be no good at this, I just know."

Healthy doubt says, "I won't find out anything unless I give it a try."
Unhealthy doubt says, "Don't bother to try. What good will it do?"

Healthy doubt says, "Nobody else has much confidence in me,
but this just might work anyway."
Unhealthy doubt says, "Everybody's right. I shouldn't do stuff
I'm no good at."

Healthy doubt says, "This might be fun, even if I'm not the best one here."
Unhealthy doubt says, "If I'm not the best, I won't have any fun."

Healthy doubt says, "I'll stick with it just a little while longer."
Unhealthy doubt says, "The first thing that goes wrong, I'm out of here."

There's a wonderful Jewish anecdote about God right after he created the world. He took a look at his creation and said, "Let's hope it works." As this list shows, healthy doubt is a lot like hope. You know that you might fall down. You know that every moment isn't going to be a triumph. But even with those doubts you move ahead. You ask the girl out who might be too good for you. You go to dance class even if it embarrasses you. You try out for crew even though every other rower outweighs you by forty pounds.

DON'T BUY IN

Unhealthy doubt is hopeless. It gives up in advance. This kind of doubt is tricky because it sounds so reasonable. It's very easy to buy into the idea that the girl you like really is too good for you, dance class really is for wimps, and those other rowers on crew really are huge. You need to step back when you have those kinds

of doubts and say, "I'm not buying into doubt. Those externals don't matter. What matters is that I go and try. I have to see for myself." In other words, you have to be a little braver than you feel, a little more confident, and a little more optimistic.

You know what? If you can go that extra step, your reality will change. You will wind up being more brave, confident, and optimistic. Doubt will be conquered, not by fighting it in a big battle, but by winning one small victory at a time.

THE SIXTH KEY TO HAPPINESS:
Make Friends with Spirit

Which profile is closest to you?

Profile #1

I know I have a soul. I go inside whenever I have a tough problem to solve, and I trust that an answer will come. I believe this is a good world and that everyone has a spiritual side. You may not see it all the time, but it's enough to make me have faith in the human race.

Profile #2

I believe in God and try to be a good person. But when I have a tough problem to solve, I work and struggle on my own. I know that life is unfair. It's sort of wishful thinking to believe that God is going to change anything.

Profile #3

God? A soul? Why are we even discussing this stuff? I will believe in these things when I see them live on TV. Otherwise, the smart thing is to look out for number one. If you don't, nobody else is going to.

Being in touch with spirit helps to get you through the difficult times in your life. Your spirit offers hope and reassurance. In that way it's like a friend, and when I think about being in contact with spirit, it's like any other friendship. You need to be able to trust in your soul. You need to be able to talk to it and bring your problems to it when things don't go so well.

MEDITATION IS RIGHT FOR YOU

We talked a little bit already about meditating. That's the main way I know of to contact spirit. You see, your soul is mixed in with the other things inside your mind. All day you experience thoughts and images, mental pictures, desires. In fact, every action you take today will have some kind of thought behind it. There's a whole drama—sometimes a circus—going on in there. Meditation allows you to step out of the drama. When everything is more settled down in your mind, then a softer, quieter part comes forward. That part is closer to spirit, and as you make friends with it, new things happen:

You begin to like it when your mind is quiet and peaceful.

You don't get as shaken up by the storms around you.

You feel like a real person, not a Ping-Pong ball tossed around by events.

You start to talk to the real you and make friends with it.

All these changes don't happen overnight, but just like any other aspect of happiness, befriending your soul will happen. All you need to do is keep at it and learn to appreciate the steps of progress that you make.

AN EASY WAY TO MEDITATE

If there's one thing in your life that should be totally easy and comfortable, it's meditation. But sometimes the pressure from the rest of your life spills over. A seventeen-year-old boy wrote:

Dear Deepak,
I am finding it hard to sit still to meditate. My mind
races around, and I feel so restless after a few minutes that
I want to jump up. What do I do?

It's okay to feel restless. You've spent a lot of years allowing your mind to race around. It's in the habit of being restless, and you can't expect it to learn to calm down overnight. Be easy on yourself, and try the following pointers:

- Lie down for a few minutes to relax and get in the mood before you meditate.

- Take a few deep breaths if your mind feels restless.

- Open your eyes and look around for a second if you feel like jumping up. Then close them and try to meditate a few minutes more.

- Make sure you always pick a quiet room and a quiet time of day to meditate. Unplug the phone and be sure that others around you know that this is your private time.

A few minutes twice a day is better than pushing yourself to sit for a longer time. Don't push at all. This is your time to make friends with a new part of yourself. You'd never want to be friends with someone at school whom you had to force yourself to like. The same is true for your friendship with your own spirit.

I once heard a spiritual teacher say that there are two ways to keep a dog close to home: You can tie it up or you can leave a little food by the back door. The first way forces it to stick around. The second way entices it by holding out something the dog likes. The soul can be attracted only in the second way, by giving it something enticing. Instead of keeping away, it will say to itself, "Oh, he's actually paying attention. He wants to know me, and it feels real." The soul is attracted to be with you in many ways. Meditation is only one of them. Include some of the activities from the sidebar "Food for Your Soul" in your daily routine.

Laughing from the heart

Listening to inspiring music

Reading inspiring books

Showing loving behavior

Being kind to yourself

Showing gentleness

Playing games that bring out the fun of life

Walking in the moonlight, gazing at the ocean

Being in a still forest

Sharing a beautiful experience with someone

Giving and helping, offering to be of service

As you can see by that list, you don't have to plunge into a strange or exotic spiritual life to be in touch with your soul. These are all everyday things that attract spirit as naturally as sugar water in a feeder attracts humming-birds. They bring out the peace and stillness, the joy and awareness, that are inside you right now, ready to show themselves.

I put laughter first on the list because of a delightful question I got from a high school junior from Brazil:

Dear Deepak,
   I am very interested in the philosophy of life, but on a beautiful day I can't help myself: I skip my religion class at our Catholic school and go dancing with my friends. I love to dance! Don't you think a person can learn as much about life from dancing as from class?

Don't show this to your parents, but yes, I do. Pure happiness, which is what dancing is all about, brings you very close to your soul. I am reminded of a story about the famous writer Gertrude Stein when she was in college. She came into class to take her philosophy final, and to her professor's surprise, she turned in her exam after two minutes and left.

On her paper she had written, "This is such a beautiful day, I don't think I can stay indoors and write about philosophy."

The professor wrote back, "You're right," and gave her an A.

KEEPING THE SOUL AWAY

I won't dwell on the opposite topic, the things that keep the soul away. Your soul isn't really a delicate hummingbird. It's eternal and cannot be hurt, no matter what you do or what anyone does to you. But the soul can be covered over, like clouds covering the sun. After four or five gloomy days in a row you stare at the grayness and say, "Is the sun ever coming back?" You know it is, but the grayness puts you in a glum mood.

If you spend too many gloomy days inside yourself, you can begin to doubt that your soul is even there. To avoid that kind of glum doubt, don't engage in harsh activity. That includes harsh music, being mean to others, hanging around with hard, tough people—that sort of thing. But distractions also keep the soul out of sight. You can't really expect to contact spirit if your head is buzzing with TV, music, and video games every free minute of the day. I'm not saying this in a mood of disapproval. Everyone has their pet distractions. But if you want to make friends with your soul, it deserves some quality attention like any other friend.

THE SEVENTH KEY TO HAPPINESS:
Make a Contribution

Which profile is closest to you?

Profile #1

I really like being helpful and giving to others. So much so that I may go into one of the helping professions, like medicine. It makes me feel good to see the happiness I can bring to others, and I am aware of how much needs to be changed in the world.

Profile #2

Helping isn't high on my list, but I pitch in when asked. I think it's good to make a contribution where you can. Maybe someday I will have to ask for help when I am in a jam, so maybe I'm building up some brownie points with God by helping someone else.

Profile #3

I don't think about making a contribution. It's not that I am so selfish, but my life is pretty full right now. Anyway, I'm not so sure one person can really make a difference. I will have more time for others once I make a good life for myself.

SHARE YOUR SPIRIT

Any time you help to increase someone's well-being, you are contributing to their life and also to everyone else's. That's because spirit is shared. When a wave rises on the ocean, it could look around and say, "I'm alone. I'm myself, and this is my ocean." But of course each wave is just one small event in the vastness of the

ocean. In the same way, your soul feels separate when in fact it is part of spirit as a whole. Wherever there is kindness and love in the world, you are invisibly benefitted. Wherever there is violence and hurt in the world, you are invisibly diminished.

I'm not asking you to believe a mystical idea. You've already experienced what it's like to have something really good happen to your family, or something really bad. I remember when I was quite small and woke up in the night to hear women crying all over the house. This was in India, and my grandfather had suddenly died in the night. Just that day he had taken me and my younger brother, Sanjiv, to the movies. We both loved him very much, and the moment he died, the whole atmosphere in the house changed. I was old enough to know what death was, but Sanjiv kept tearfully asking where Baba had gone and when he was coming back. Everyone was very upset, for something dreadful had happened, and it was happening to all of us.

YOU ARE A PART OF EVERYTHING

When you watch the TV news and see war unfolding around the world, that same feeling of "It's happening to all of us" is present. Your spirit is helped or hurt by events far away. I think it's important to do something with your life that helps everyone's well-being, because that's how you show that you care about the whole human family.

Alfred Stieglitz was one of the century's greatest photographers, and he also reached out and helped many other artists. As a child he showed a very special attitude toward life. His parents noticed that on snowy winter nights he would slip out the back door for a few moments and then return silently without saying why. They soon discovered that there was a homeless man who camped out in the alley, and their son was giving him some of his own allowance.

"That's wonderful," Stieglitz's parents said. "You're doing good for another person."

The boy looked a little baffled. "Don't you see? I'm doing it for myself," he said.

Some people have a different idea of what the word *contribution* means. They might contribute to one political party so that it can beat another. But a spiritual contribution doesn't take sides; it works to help the whole human spirit. Some people make contributions to charity, which is certainly a good thing to do. But to me, a spiritual contribution is personal; it involves human contact and not just a number written on a piece of paper. Your contribution doesn't have to be big. Think about doing any of the following:

- Don't you know someone who might be lonely? Visit them.

- Don't you know someone who could use a friend? Be that friend.

- Don't you know someone who's falling behind in class? Offer to tutor them.

- Don't you see homeless people on the street, including kids your own age? Help them by working at a shelter.

- Don't you know that many children have few advantages in life? Become a big brother or sister to a disadvantaged child.

- Don't you see a way to help your own little brother or sister? Act on your good impulses and be a better big brother or sister.

You aren't changing the world when you do any of these things, yet in a way you are. At the invisible level you've added a bit toward the well-being of the human soul. Your contribution touches everyone even when you seem to be touching one person at a time.

THE EIGHTH KEY TO HAPPINESS:
Avoid Violence

Which profile is closest to you?

Profile #1

I feel enough peace with myself that it's easy to be peaceful toward others. I don't have anger and resentment that I keep hidden. It's okay for me to tell someone else when they have made me mad, and I take responsibility for its being my anger and not their fault. I look for ways to forgive, and my natural urge is to find a way to settle conflicts.

Profile #2

I don't go looking for trouble, and so my life runs pretty peacefully. I do have a temper, and I can hold grudges when somebody makes me mad. It's not my fault if I resent others; it's their fault for doing the wrong thing. It makes me feel good to forgive somebody, but I don't go out of my way to do it. They have to come to me first.

Profile #3

I can remember getting into quite a few fights, and I still have a temper. I don't put up with stuff. You better know that if you cross me, you'll have trouble on your hands. Things can get pretty rough at home—at least one of my parents has a hot temper. It bothers me that I hold grudges a long time, but what else am I supposed to do?

WHY ARE WE SO VIOLENT?

One of the biggest questions in life is whether human beings are born to be violent. In a typical year, like 2003, there are thirty wars going on somewhere around the world. In the entire history of civilization it has been computed that 92 percent of the time human beings were at war. No one needs statistics to prove that crime has been present 100 percent of the time. Personal violence is the root cause of war, and even though you and I may consider ourselves peaceful, we've probably gotten into a fight at one time or another, egged on a fistfight at school, rooted for one side to win a war, or gotten into hotheaded arguments.

So violence is with us all. It mars the human spirit every day. Can we do without it? That's a totally personal question, because violence has to end one person at a time. Avoiding violence means avoiding all its disguises, too. I imagine you didn't beat anybody up today, but what about these forms of hidden violence?

Violence in Disguise

Picking an argument with a family member

Speaking ill of someone behind their back

Wishing that something bad will happen to someone

Judging someone to be evil

Rooting for the bad guys to be wiped out

Cheering on a war

Wanting criminals to be punished to the max

Mistreating or neglecting an animal

Insulting someone

Using a racial slur

Having contempt for a whole group of people

You might not think these are violent acts. You might even be in the habit of having bad thoughts or using ethnic slurs with the vague notion that it's okay as long as you don't carry things too far. But if you've ever stood around a bonfire, you know that throwing a log on the fire isn't the only way to get it to burn higher. All it takes is a little extra breeze. When you indulge in these hidden forms of violence, you are adding to the breeze. You haven't actually hurt someone physically, yet you have made it easier for that to happen.

BE ON THE LOOKOUT

It takes a little vigilance to avoid violence. Think about what it's like to get into a really heated debate. Let's say you've gotten into a political debate with somebody. Isn't it easy to cross the line and sneer at the other side, to trash their opinion and make them feel as if only you are the good person? One sees that kind of political fight on television every night. Yet it is a form of violence. You are verbally and mentally trying to wipe somebody out. Making someone out to be a bad person is uncalled-for aggression. At the very least, two people can have opposite opinions and yet be equally good people.

A STORY OF SELF-DEFENSE

There is a difference between aggression and self-defense, however. When I was a starving intern fresh out of medical school, I lived in a rough part of Boston with my young wife and newborn baby girl. One night I was alone in the apartment with my daughter. There was a pounding at the door, and without warning a man barged in. He was acting very violent, and without thinking, I picked up a baseball bat. He charged at me, and I swung at his head, knocking him out. When the police came, they discovered that he had a long criminal record, and there was no question that I had a right to defend myself.

A TWIST TO THE STORY

But that incident must have preyed on my mind. Even though I had used aggression to defend myself against violence, I felt a deep sorrow for what had happened. Almost thirty years later I left a lecture hall by the back door and was walking down a dark alley. Three youths approached me, pulled out a gun, and demanded my wallet. I froze for a second, then I said, "You can have my money, but I need my wallet. Don't use that gun, because you will be hurting yourself much more than you'll hurt me."

These were kids no more than sixteen or seventeen, and I could sense that they had not yet become completely bad. The one holding the gun trembled, and I could see that my words had had an effect. I did wind up handing over some money but keeping my wallet. As they ran away, I had the sense that these kids got to see their own violence through someone else's eyes. Maybe that will make a difference in their own lives. For myself, I felt that I had helped to restore the balance. I had committed violence long ago, and now I might have reduced it by a fraction.

This tale isn't about putting yourself in harm's way. I just hope you will look at the list of disguised violence and make a good effort to stop doing anything that fits your current behavior. Never again use a slur, even in jest. Don't root for war and fall into the trap of thinking that a whole nation or group of people is evil. No matter how angry you get at someone, it is a truism that every person on Earth has someone who loves them. If a person is worth someone's love, they aren't worth your hatred. It's as simple as that. Violence in all its subtle forms ends with you and every other spiritual person who is willing to walk away.

THE NINTH KEY TO HAPPINESS:
Cherish Nature

Which profile is closest to you?

Profile #1

I am close to nature. I know that I am part of Mother Earth, who deserves love and respect. None of us would be alive without the nourishment of our planet, and whenever I can, I get out into nature so that I can appreciate it firsthand.

Profile #2

I know the earth has problems, and I care. But there are a lot of other problems a lot closer to home. I figure the planet has always been here and always will be. Maybe somebody will figure out what to do about global warming. In the meantime, I enjoy going to the beach or the mountains, but mostly my life is spent at home and at the mall.

Profile #3

I think all this alarm about the planet has gone too far. We need oil and gas, that's the reality. I'm not cutting down the rain forest, so it's not my problem. My kids may seriously have to worry long ahead in the future. For right now, I have television and the Internet. Nature feels pretty far away, frankly.

FIRST, AN APOLOGY

My generation has to apologize to your generation. We did more to harm the planet than anyone born before us. This isn't because my generation is made up of people with bad instincts. We have the same instincts as the human beings who came before us. But unfortunately, modern life gave us undreamed-of powers to do harm. As a result, the earth has been stripped of its treasures as never before, and its most delicate ecosystems are in peril.

Your generation must cherish the planet once more. It's not possible to be healthy in an unhealthy world. You may never dive under the sea to gaze in amazement at a coral reef, but the fact that a third of the world's coral reefs are dying is part of your life now, along with the dying rain forests and global warming. There is no better time to learn to love this planet.

CHERISHING THE EARTH

The only healthy way to be on this planet is to see yourself as a brief flicker in the infinite progress of life and yet as a cherished child of nature. The best reason to cherish the earth is that it cherishes you. Here are the dying words of a Blackfoot Indian chief named Isapwo Muksika Crowfoot:

> What is life? It is the flash of a firefly in the night. It is the breath of a buffalo in the wintertime. It is the little shadow which runs across the grass and loses itself in the sunset.

I can see each image and feel the chief's love and wisdom, which came to him from the earth. No other creature except man is capable of loving all other creatures. Yet no other creature is

capable of doing so much harm. You and everyone your age will have to make decisions based on sympathy for the earth or cruelty toward it.

Which is more important, doubling the price of gasoline or doubling the pollution in the air?

Which will harm you more, paying extra taxes or dirty factory smokestacks?

Is it more important to water our lawns three times a week or to send river water to another country, like Mexico?

My generation has asked these questions without successfully answering them. We wanted to answer without selfishness, but ultimately good intentions weren't enough. So there has to be a change of attitude that goes as deep as the soul. You would never harm your family just for cheap gas, and in time you will have to realize that you are harming the human family by insisting on cheap gas. It's not simple, because global issues force us to see the world through the eyes of strangers from other countries. I think the answers must begin with a love for nature. Loving nature is like loving your own body, because in the larger picture the air is the breathing of your lungs, the forests are the fiber of your muscles, and the ocean is the water in every cell. You came from these beginnings as surely as you came out of your mother.

THE TENTH KEY TO HAPPINESS:
Never Stop Growing

Which profile is closest to you?

Profile #1

I believe that my life can be exceptional. I embrace new things every day—new knowledge, new experiences, new hopes for my future. I can't wait to grow up, so that I can "grow on" for the rest of my life. The people I admire most have adventurous spirits.

Profile #2

I look forward to having a good life. I think family is the most important thing, and I intend to provide for my own family one day with a good house and all kinds of great things. The people I admire the most have done this and more. They have great material accomplishments to their credit.

Profile #3

It's tough to be where I am right now, and what I most hope for is to get out of school and out on my own. I want to stop following someone else's rules. This is my life, and when I get the chance, I'm going to do whatever I want. The people I admire the most are rockers and rebels, the kind who don't let anyone tell them what to do.

GROWING IS PECULIAR

Growing starts out as something you can't help doing. Babies and young children don't think about growing; the whole process is built into their genes. Did you know that just before birth a baby is growing a million new nerve connections per minute? Or that a single liver cell, something you'll never see or think about, has to perform more than fifty operations perfectly? Or that the storm of chemical activity in one cell erupts with a new reaction about every one hundred thousandth of a second? The most complex object in the universe, the human body, has to grow on automatic

because none of us, even the most gifted genius, could figure out how to build one.

But gradually things change, and by the time you get out of your teenage years, growing becomes a choice. The master control is given over to you. Your body and mind have played their automatic software; the genes have done their infinitely complex work. There's no ribbon-cutting ceremony, but in fact your genes are turning to you right now and saying, "This is yours to drive. Where do you want to go? What do you intend to do?"

If I could answer my genes, I'd say, "I want to grow forever." These years are really the turning point. You can use this incredible genetic gift for anything you want. Most people use it to stop growing, which is sad. Instead of surfing that tidal wave of progress that has been moving forward for twenty years, they say to themselves, "Let's slow down. The adventure is over." In other words, they become settled, comfortable adults with a lot of habits.

SHARKS AND CATTLE

Habit is just another word for "training your mind to follow a groove." Here are two examples that caught my attention years ago, one from an aquarium full of sharks, the other from a cattle range in Montana. As you probably know, sharks are perpetually restless creatures that must keep swimming to stay alive. The ones I heard about prowled their tank every hour, swimming from one end to the other, almost touching the glass wall of the tank before veering off.

One day their keeper tried an experiment and moved the wall a few feet away. But instead of swimming up to the new barrier, the sharks turned just before they hit the old wall, which wasn't even there. This story says a lot about our own habits. We stay inside of invisible barriers because we assume that they exist. What if they don't? What if you have a much bigger tank to swim in? You'll never know if you train yourself to follow a narrow set of habits, because these will act like invisible barriers.

The other story is about keeping cattle on the ranch. Cattle like to graze wherever they can wander, and the ranches in Montana are too vast to fence in. Long ago the ranchers learned that cattle won't cross a road that has a metal grate in it, because their hooves get caught in the grate. This technique worked very well, but then someone discovered a clever improvement. Instead of installing a real grate in the road, they painted a picture of a grate, and the cattle, seeing that, took it for the real thing. They didn't want their hooves caught in the grate, so they stayed on the other side of the road permanently.

Our habits are also like that. Once we feel hurt by an experience, we don't return to it. We are spooked like cattle, and the minute we get near anything that smells of our old hurt or failure or humiliation, we veer away.

HOW TO KEEP GROWING

If you want to grow for the rest of your life, you'll have to overcome both these tendencies: the tendency to stay inside old walls, and the tendency to shy away from experiences when they don't turn out perfectly. As a wise person once said, "Life isn't about being perfect. It's about being better every day."

The kind of habits that hold you back from growing aren't simple things like brushing your teeth every morning or always catching your favorite TV show. I'm referring to psychological habits, the kind that keep life from expanding. See if you fit any of the sketches listed in the sidebar "The Habit Trap."

We all fall into these traps at one time or another. But it's

THE HABIT TRAP: HOW THE MIND GETS STUCK IN A GROOVE

Trap #1:
Blindly Opinionated

I make up my mind fast. Once I do, I don't look any further. My opinion is my opinion. Don't try to change it.

Trap #2:
The Conformist

My buddies and I know what we think. We know what kinds of things we like and don't like. I keep with the group's ideas. I think others envy me because I know I belong.

Trap #3:
The Black Sheep

I'm a rebel, so I reject whatever somebody tells me just because they are in charge. If my father thinks something—or anyone else his age—it's automatically wrong.

Trap #4:
The Little Mouse

I steer away from big topics. I don't follow the world of politics or major issues of the day. My life is simple. I keep to the things that concern me every day.

good to be on the lookout in case you find that one is really sinking in and becoming your pet habit. For more than eighty years fans mourned the Red Sox and always expected them to lose out on the World Series—that would be pessimism—but that didn't help them win (which they finally did in 2004). And what if you believe that you'll never find the right person to marry? That's also pessimistic, and your gloomy expectations hurt your chances of finding love. Each of these traps is like that. There's no harm in seeing the world through rose-colored glasses if you are planning the senior prom and want it to be the prettiest event you've ever seen, but what if someone came to you with a drug problem? Then smiling and saying "Oh, it'll all turn out okay. You're still a beautiful person" isn't right.

STAY OUT OF THE TRAP

I ran across a brilliant article on advertising. It talked about how to get the most people to buy what you have to sell, whether it's cars, soft drinks, or shaving cream. There was one secret to all of them: *Make the consumer think he's a rebel.* Show a tough, macho guy riding off on a Harley, and the viewer will want to be that guy (of course, this works only for males, really). Now put a bottle of soda in his hand—or a video game, or give him a certain pair of jeans—and presto! *Drinking this cola makes you a rebel!* It doesn't really, though. All it does is invite the viewer to share in Trap #3, the Black Sheep. The writer of the article didn't talk much about female consumers, but the hypnotic image for them is romance and glamour. In other words, Trap #6, Rose-Colored Glasses, which make you a supermodel if you buy this diet cola. Funny how the same soft drink can make you either macho or glamorous, but such is the power of habit. You're not expected to think, only to respond.

If you really want to grow for a lifetime, start rejecting these habit traps now. It's the best way to keep growing, because the only mind that keeps growing isn't the brilliant mind, but the free mind. It's a gift you and only you can give yourself.

Trap #5:
The Cynic

Why believe in anything? I know in advance that most people are either lying or fooling themselves. Only a sucker believes that goodness prevails. The smart people have figured out life in advance.

Trap #6:
Rose-Colored Glasses

Everything's going to turn out fine, just you wait and see. I don't bother about all the problems people see everywhere. Life always has problems, but if you are patient, the best will happen in the end.

Trap #7:
The Pessimist

I hate to be blindsided, so I expect the worst. If I'm wrong and something good happens, well, great. Thanks for the surprise. But I've been burned too many times, so now I protect myself.

Relationships

The spiritual rule about relationships is simple:
Everything is connected. This rule is so important because it cancels out a lot of what our emotions tell us. Emotionally it's a lot easier to be out for yourself. You want others to satisfy whatever it is you want. You feel different, set apart. In your worst moments you feel completely alone.

But it's not really like that.

Everyone harbors a fantasy about being the most important person in the world, or always being right and never contradicted. This fantasy works when you are a baby, because at that age your mother and father rush to meet your every need. By the time you are a teen, however, the world has changed. Parents say no a lot. Teachers make demands that you have to fulfill if you want to move ahead. Friends divide into cliques that only grow more divided over time. The fantasy of being number one fades, and what replaces it?

Relationships—and all the work that goes into them.

AN EASIER WAY

I'd like to show you that spirit can make these relationships much less work and much more fulfilling. At the level of the soul your fantasy comes true. You are number one, but at the same time you make room for the needs of all those other people who want to be number one also.

I'm sure you've heard someone say, "I'm not in a relationship right now." But is that really possible? Our whole life is spent in relationships. Think about the simplest of sentences, "I am." No matter what word follows, you've named a relationship.

"I am a son or a daughter." That's a relationship with your family.

"I am in school." That's a relationship with your peers and your town.

"I am captain of the football team." That's a relationship with your team and your fans.

"I am from Ohio." That's a relationship to a state and a country.

You can begin to see why the spiritual rule of relationships—*everything is connected*—is true. An invisible web holds the world together. Every person on Earth is part of it; every living creature depends upon it. With that in mind, look at the following questions:

Dear Deepak,
   What do you think about premarital sex?
   Should parents spank their children?
   Where will the world be in twenty-five years?
   What do you think about interracial dating?
   Do you like everyone you work with?
   Why are my parents so crazy?

All these questions came from different young people, but they could have been from one. I remember asking all these things myself, and yet they come down to the same question: "How am I supposed to relate?"

If you can answer that question, the smaller ones become much easier. Sex, parents, school, race—all these issues become easier once you realize that everyone is connected. Because then

it is never "us versus them." It's never who's the bad guy and who's the good guy. You begin to see that there's good and bad in everyone, and we're all in this together.

FIGURING IT ALL OUT

The pressure to figure out relationships gets much stronger in the teen years. You worry about being seen with the right crowd, about fitting in and avoiding criticism. As a result, a lot of teens make short-term choices. They fall for the "us versus them" mentality in the desperate hope that this attitude will offer some much needed protection.

My friends are cool. Those guys aren't.

I'm a junior. Don't talk to me, because you're only a freshman.

Our team is going to kill your team.

Our school is the best. Their school is the pits.

Don't you hear these statements—or very close equivalents—every day? They illustrate the "us versus them" mentality. People who talk like this aren't usually being mean for the sake of being mean. They want to belong. They want to feel good about who they are. They want sharp lines to exist between good and bad. In time they might even believe in those things. But it's not the spiritual way to see the world; it's not how your soul sees you or anybody else.

Everyone is connected, which means that we are all the same spiritually. That's the soul's view, and I believe it's the best way to deal with relationships. You weren't put here on this earth to sit in judgment over who is cool or superior or good. You are here to contribute to the delicate web of humanity. By making connections stronger in any way you can, you are giving hope for the future.

IS THIS YOUR FANTASY?

There are other fantasies that grip teens. One is this: "If only I can find the right man (or woman), then all my troubles will be solved." Another is this: "If I build a beautiful family in a beautiful house, my life will be perfect." A lot of effort is put into both fantasies, not just by teens, but by our whole society. Well, I was fortunate and married my first love. We built a beautiful family, but that was only the start of fulfilling many other needs. Needs can be filled only through relationships.

Let's look again at those teen questions, and others, with that in mind.

When Is Sex Right?

Q: What do you think about premarital sex?

A: What I think is just another adult's opinion. What do you think about sex among your friends and the other kids at school? Now we've taken the question into the area where it counts. You are going to live by the values you believe in, and what are they? Adults seem to think that sex is dangerous among teens because they have no control over "raging hormones." Yet surveys show that teens split off into groups over sex. If you have friends who are already having sex, you won't hold the same values as someone whose friends don't have sex. But whatever group you belong to, 80 percent of teens say that having sex when you're too young isn't cool. It makes you a loser, to use their own word.

I don't believe this is about being cool or being a loser. As a teen, you feel a sexual drive and must come to terms with it. Which means that sex comes up and you have to make a decision. These are the questions you need to ask:

Will I feel good about my decision tomorrow?

Will I keep my dignity and reputation?

How do other kids whom I admire act?

Which adults seem to have the best advice on this subject?

By asking these questions, you are relating. You aren't just stuck by yourself in the backseat of a car or on a bed before your parents come home from work. It becomes hard to resist that other person who is saying, "Come on, let's do it. It will feel good." In the context of your whole life feeling good for half an hour may have a sorrowful payback later.

So get in the habit of asking the questions above. You'll find it easier to say no. The day will come when you can ask these same questions and come up with a different answer: "Yes, my friends, my age group at school, and everyone I trust will be glad that I am going to experience sex." When you can say that, you have a good chance to experience the beautiful side of sex and not just a brief rush of excitement.

BAD REASONS FOR SEX

In any case, if you find yourself pressured to have sex, always say no. If someone is going to strip you of your dignity, always say no. If someone is going to talk behind your back and label you as loose, always say no. If someone asks for unprotected sex, always say no.

But here's the hard one. If you are tempted to have sex so that someone will like you and make you feel more secure, absolutely say no. You won't get what you're hoping for, and often you will get the exact opposite.

How Much Discipline?

Q: Should parents spank their children?

A: This is really a question that I'd expect from parents, but I think it came from a teen because teens are thinking about the future. You are starting to relate more to the adult world, where parental decisions will be yours. Let's broaden this question a little and ask, "How much discipline should parents exert at home?" To me, the rules here are pretty straightforward.

WHEN DISCIPLINE FAILS

If you demean with punishment, you've gone too far. A child should never be humiliated or made to feel unloved.

If you remove a child's dignity, you've gone too far. A child should never be made to feel like a bad person. We all make mistakes, but we remain good people nonetheless.

If you try to force good behavior, you will fail. The best discipline sends a message, "I am disappointed in your behavior. I expected better." Trying to force a child to follow certain values only instills resentment and rebellion.

Discipline without love is cruelty. Every parent who has ever struck a child in anger feels guilty afterward. In your heart you know whether you lashed out in frustration or to let off steam or because you didn't know any better way to react. Those aren't acceptable excuses. Punishment should be a reluctant choice that is made out of love and caring for a child.

As for what I think is fair during the teenage years, I don't believe in tough love. So-called tough love is like shutting the barn door after the horse is gone. Real love has already failed. Real love is always the answer, and it must develop over time, starting very early. Real love makes a kid feel worthy and respected. Real love makes a kid feel safe and wanted. Real love draws boundaries but doesn't guard them with fear.

CHANGING THE PAST

You need to see that your actions form a pattern. Something you do today is connected to what you did yesterday. Parents discipline according to how their children have acted in the past. So don't isolate yourself and try to cut your parents off. This isn't "us versus them." Change your pattern, and then your actions will speak for themselves. Ask yourself about your past:

- Do you have a habit of ignoring requests from your parents?

- Do you tune them out?

- Do you say you will do something just to get them off your back?

- Do you resent having to do your fair share around the house?

- Do you just want them to leave you alone?

All these things will cause any parent to step up the discipline. Why? Because you are letting down your half of the relationship, and they see no alternative but to impose more discipline. It really comes down to that. They aren't on your case. They don't want to turn you into a military recruit. What's happened is that you have disconnected from them. As soon as you disconnect, you violate the spiritual rule of relationships, which is that everything is connected.

MAKE THE CONNECTION

If you reconnect, things will get better. Your parents will sense the lowered stress and tension, and once that happens, they won't feel a need to try to get your attention through rules and schedules.

So how do you reconnect?

You have to make today different from yesterday. Your parents have an image of you built up over the years. You have an image of them built up over the years. It's these images that have gotten stuck. In reality you are more than an image, and so are they. So by acting more real and human, you can get unstuck.

It's human to talk and communicate. It's not human to tune people out.

It's human to be interested in others. It's not human to be in your own fortress of solitude.

It's human to care. It's not human to be apathetic.

It's human to cooperate. It's not human to throw up obstacles and resistance.

Put yourself on the human side of the equation again. Yes, I know that I have loaded the word *human* here. There are many human beings who are apathetic, uncooperative, obstructive, and isolated, but that's not the side of human nature you want to encourage. I think you can find one thing to do today that fits each point:

You can take ten minutes to talk to each parent alone.

You can communicate one thing that interests you.

You can show interest in one thing they care about.

You can do one chore without being asked.

You can find one rule that you have stubbornly resisted and tell them that you feel like cooperating.

Don't feel as if you are giving in to the enemy by doing these things. You aren't. It may be that on some issues you are more in the right than your parents. It may be that they need to change as much as you do—or at least some. But there's only one way to get to a fair balance. You have to soften from your side and then learn to negotiate over unfair rules. Disobedience will only harden the battle lines further. At the soul level your parents have perfect love for you; at the soul level you have perfect love for them. With this in mind, you have a basis for hope—every situation can be brought closer to the spiritual ideal.

The World Is a Mirror

Q: Where will the world be in twenty-five years?
A: Not being a psychic, I can't tell you where the world will be, but I can tell you *what* it will be. It will be a reflection of the people in it. The world is a mirror. It always has been and always will be. Nothing exists in it except what we humans put there. For me this is a spiritual truth that takes a lot of adjusting. I'm tempted to think that the good things that happen to me are due to my wonderful actions, while the bad things are unfair or accidental.

But I can't deserve the good and not deserve the bad. In truth I am relating on many levels all the time, and since life is really complicated, I have learned to trust the reflections I see around me. Reflections don't lie. If people stay away from you, there's a reason, and the reason begins with you. It's not fate; it's not those horrible kids who are such losers and snobs. If you lose three jobs in a row, there's a reason, and it begins with you. It's not that awful boss and the impossible working conditions.

CAN YOU SEE YOUR REFLECTIONS?

Now, some people heartily disagree with this view. They don't see any reflections. They are right and the world is just unfair. Life itself is unfair. You can take that position and try to live it. We all have an ego. We'd all like to be right all the time. The harder road by far is to look honestly at the reflections you're getting. Here are some hard things that some young people suddenly realized:

I always thought my dad was awful, very mean and unfair. Then one day I went to a meeting where he was in charge. He really got people to pay attention, and they voted for the things he wanted. It was really surprising to see him in that role. I had to ask myself why he didn't treat me that way and whether part of the problem was me.

I am outgoing and speak my mind. I think of myself as cheerful, but other kids say I am stuck up and unapproachable. That never made sense. Then I saw a videotape of a birthday party where someone filmed me without my knowing it. I saw myself looking down my nose and sometimes saying really sharp things. I had thought they were funny, but they weren't. This was a wake-up call for me to change. I totally hadn't seen what others saw so easily.

I was watching TV with some friends, and we were just hanging out. Then I went into the other room for a few minutes. I heard them all laughing and sounding very loose and happy. Then it hit me: They weren't like that when I was there. I asked myself if anyone ever laughed and relaxed around me, and I didn't like the answer I was getting. I think I have to loosen up.

WHAT IS KARMA?

In India the idea that the world is a mirror is known as karma. *Karma* has many meanings. Basically the word just means "action" in Sanskrit. But karma is a special kind of action, the kind that balances out the good and bad of our lives. In other words, karma carries out the maxim that what you sow, so shall you reap. I don't want you to adopt this new word, but I would like you to consider that if the idea of "Good brings good, and bad brings bad" has existed for thousands of years—not just in India, but in every culture—maybe there's something to it. The world is not just a mirror, but a karmic mirror. It shows you where you need to do more good by bringing bad reflections.

This is a deep topic, and there is lots of controversy around it. Some people are dead set in believing that they are victims who

deserve nothing bad that ever happens to them. Some people accept the scientific tenet that the world is a place of random actions that have nothing to do with good and bad. You will have to keep thinking about that for your whole life. I can speak only as someone who has tried to learn a lesson from every bad reflection, turning it inward to see where I could be better. I don't make karma a heavy thing. I certainly don't use it to say, "Oh, I deserve all this bad stuff that is coming my way." I'd call that attitude passive and fatalistic. Instead, I look in the mirror every day, and frankly, although I don't always like what I see there, I try to have the character to admit that what I see is true. There I am, warts and all. The good news is that I can work to change every reflection. Karma isn't a cage that shuts you in. It's a clue to where the key is that lets you out.

Follow Your Heart

Q: What do you think about interracial dating?

A: I think that the person you want to be with is the person you want to be with. Two forces are always at work here. One force brings people into closer connection. The other force tries to keep people apart. Usually the second force has a lot of anger and prejudice on its side. The teen who asked this question informed me that his parents had strong religious convictions that made it wrong to date someone from another race. Well, there used to be religious reasons not to dance or listen to music, not to let women out of the house, not to have sex except to procreate children, and so forth. Supposedly those rules came from God, and yet somehow in almost every modern society they were allowed to change.

The level of ignorance in this world is sometimes helped by religion and sometimes not. You have to use your own heart to decide. I'd say that if you side with the first force, the one that brings people into closer connection, you will have a happier time personally, and you will be riding the wave of the future.

Liking Everybody

Q: Do you like everyone you work with?

A: My answer is yes, the people I work with are all wonderful, but you don't have to like everybody. You can't expect to blend perfectly with every person you meet in life. However, you can give everyone the benefit of the doubt. We're all connected, and if you decide too rashly on whom to like, you are automatically disconnecting yourself. That's never a good idea. You will miss out on a lot, and you will never see how much each person has to offer. At the soul level you are saying yes to everybody. Try to see the positive in each person so that you can get closer to the reality of your soul. Don't fake it and don't strain. The great Indian saint Sri Ramakrishna was asked if he loved every person he ever met, including all the bad people and rough customers. He wisely replied, "I know that everyone is my brother and should be loved like a brother. But some brothers I can love from a distance."

The Problem with Parents

Q: Why are my parents so crazy?

A: An excellent question. It has been asked by every breathing child at some point in his or her life. The reason parents are so crazy is that they aren't you. You have crossed over the line where you easily blend into your parents' lives, and that is as it should be. You will always be connected to your parents. Even if you run away from home or get so mad that you never speak to them again or wind up losing your parents too early, that connection is forever. It was forged invisibly by the thousands of hours that you paid attention to them and they paid attention to you.

So, what is the right connection that will make you happy and them less crazy?

TAKING CARE

I think I have at least one simple answer: Start to take care of each other. You are moving past the age of needing them to take care of you. Independence is on your mind and grows stronger every day. Well, independent people take care of others. They don't shoot off into isolation, thinking only of themselves. Have you thought about showing your independence by taking care of your parents? This means all kinds of things, like those listed in the sidebar "How to Tame a Wild Parent."

I bet you've never heard anyone suggest that teenagers should begin to take care of their parents. I think that's because we all think in terms of material things like money and food and a roof over your head. Your parents don't need those things from you. But at the soul level you are equal. It's only during the early years that adults must act out the part of being in charge. We have to be strong and responsible because that's how children are raised. But at a certain point equality returns. You will one day look at your parents from the same level.

HOW TO TAME A WILD PARENT

Do not give them reason to worry

See things from their point of view

Give them the benefit of the doubt

Make housework a little easier

Be responsible for your own schedule

Take care of your health

Make a few sacrifices of time and effort

Show that you care about the sacrifices they've made for you

It's a wonderful change, a kind of growth that brings a new kind of love and respect into the family. I don't want you to jump the gun. Enjoy being a teenager; let your parents take care of you as much as they want and you can tolerate. But realize too that you are an equal soul. You can begin to live that realization by taking care of them a little. That's how two souls show love for each other, by sharing the same soul journey together. Which, if you think about it, is exactly what you and your parents have been doing since the day you were born.

The Golden Rule of Friendship

Q: I was really attracted to this one girl at school, and now we've started to hang out. But all her other friends seem to have a lot more money than me. They spend hours shopping, and there's no way I could afford to do that. I know that they judge everyone by how much money they have. What should I do?

A: There's a golden rule of friendship, which is equality. At the soul level we are all equal. Being a friend means getting close to someone's soul, and two friends need to feel that they are equal. Otherwise the sense of inequality will always create tension. In your case, you don't want to be friends with everyone this girl knows. You just want to be friends with her. So when you feel the moment is right, take her aside and say you're not that interested in shopping. Don't bring up money or how embarrassed you feel about not being able to keep up with her crowd. Make this girl your personal friend based on things you can share as equals.

You'll never have enough money to impress people who judge others only by how well off they are. It's not possible to share your soul with people who are that superficial. Do your best to ignore their attitude and concentrate on your friend. If it turns out that she is too much like them and judges others by how much they spend, then she is the one who hasn't followed the golden rule of friendship. That would be sad, but it's not your responsibility. Your responsibility is to follow the golden rule yourself.

Hard Time Making Friends

Q: I have a hard time making friends. What should I do?

A: Making friends is harder now than it used to be. Many families move several times while their children are still young. Few of us grow up in a small town where everybody knows everybody else. And it's said that schools are more divided than ever into cliques. What all this means is that you can't take friends for granted. You have to focus your attention on making a friend instead of just waiting for one to come along.

So, how do you do that? How do you make a stranger into a friend? Here are some tried-and-true behaviors that seem to work:

Listen more than you speak.

Notice someone's good points and mention them.

Show that you admire the other person.

Accept who the other person is.

Be kind and thoughtful.

Anticipate something the other person might like and then offer it.

I realize that there is one big drawback to all of these points: You actually have to know the person at least a little bit before you can use any of them. And for most kids that's the toughest part—getting to know someone who could reject you, no matter how nice you are or how friendly you act. Just know that you

aren't alone in feeling uncomfortable during those first moments of saying hello. There are no magical ways to skirt the awkwardness that might arise.

KEEP IT SIMPLE

In a way nothing beats simplicity. Walk right up and say, "I'd like to be friends." If you are afraid that this is too bold for you, then think of a natural compliment that will open the conversation, such as noticing something about how the person is dressed. Saying "That's a cool haircut" or "Where did you get that cool bike?" immediately shows that you admire that person. Don't do the opposite and talk about yourself first. Too often we are tempted to say things like "I have that same bike" or "I got that same shirt last week." Putting yourself first in the conversation is usually an automatic turnoff. You're asking someone else to admire you, but it won't work until they really have a good reason to.

I believe in the direct approach to making new friends, but you risk being rejected that way. Fear of rejection is probably the number one reason teenagers—and most adults—would rather be safe alone than risk the chance of being humiliated. And it only takes being burned once—having someone turn their back and walk away as if you are an insect they almost stepped on—to feel very scared from that moment on. Once burned, twice shy, as the saying goes.

So here are a few thoughts to help you bolster yourself for that awkward first moment.

BOOSTING YOUR CONFIDENCE

Other kids are just as shy and self-conscious as you are,
even if they don't show it.

Anyone who rejects you isn't likely to turn into much of a friend.

You have a lot to offer. If someone doesn't want to be
a friend, it's their loss.

The worst you can imagine almost never happens. It's just an energy of
fear, and fear isn't always right, no matter how convincing it is.

There's so much to learn from each of these sentences that you will be able to spend a lifetime and never really run out of lessons. But for now just use them as simple reminders. You are not alone. Everyone wants friends, and everyone finds it hard to make them.

Not Good Enough

Q: I am so self-conscious that the people I want to make friends with scare me the most. I reject myself in advance. What can I do?

A: Why do you reject yourself? Almost always it's because you see yourself through someone else's eyes. In your head you hear someone's voice saying, "You're not good enough," and so you think everybody must share that opinion. But really, can anyone see themselves through anyone else's eyes? It's hard enough to see yourself through your own. (And believe me, everyone is looking at themselves all the time. You aren't alone in this.)

HOW TO SEE YOURSELF

Here's a new way to see yourself. Whatever the situation, when you feel insecure or inferior or just painfully shy, tell yourself this:

"I am a work in progress." I think that's one of the best things you can tell yourself, because it's true. Your time is coming. One day you are going to blossom. What is strong about you is only going to get stronger. What embarrasses you or makes you feel inferior can be improved—sometimes the worst things just melt away. You could find yourself in a place where quiet, shy people are seen as attractive, and then someone who really loves you may spot you sitting there, like an overlooked flower. For now just remember that nothing is finished: You are truly a work in progress.

Bursting His Bubble

Q: I have this friend who sits in the back of class all day and doodles. He doesn't care about grades because he says he's going to be a rich and famous cartoonist one day. The problem is he's no good! How can I tell him to stop throwing away his life?

A: Let's put your question a different way. Aren't you asking me for a pin so you can burst your friend's bubble? Is that a good thing to do to a friend, even if you are right? Lots of people will be there to tell him he's not that good. The world never runs out of critics. But a friend is different. He's there to support

you. If things really get out of hand—if you see him doodling all night on a date—then sure, you might step in.

But I bet you are pretty good in class, or else you wouldn't feel so concerned about your friend's future. Maybe your energies would be better used to get him interested in class. Pick the subject that you like the best and share your enthusiasm. That's a good way to jump-start a friend who is having a hard time finding any inner motivation. And if your friend says, "Thanks, but no thanks," then know you've done the best you can and continue to be supportive whatever he chooses to do.

Being a True Friend

Q: How will I know when I have found a true friend?

A: A true friend is someone you can hold very close to your soul. You can tell such a friend by how he or she behaves in certain situations. You have to go through good times and bad times together. That's also how you can tell if you are being a true friend.

That means you usually can't tell your true friends in advance. But there are things that work to keep a friendship together that will help you out all your life. If I were making a list of how my best friends behaved, ten things would matter the most to me.

What a True Friend Is: Ten Qualities to Look For

1. A true friend listens to you when you need it most, not just when it's convenient.

2. A true friend feels happy for the good things in your life, even when she doesn't get anything for herself.

3. A true friend tells you the truth when it counts.

4. A true friend accepts who you are without judging you.

5. A true friend is someone you can tell a secret to without being afraid he will spread it around.

6. A true friend loves you even though you aren't perfect.

7. A true friend inspires you.

8. A true friend doesn't care what others say about you.

9. A true friend respects you.

10. A true friend lives in your heart like a part of yourself.

Now, I don't expect one person to live up to all ten of these things. If I had ten true friends and each one embodied just one of these qualities, I would consider myself very blessed. Let's look at them one at a time.

1. A true friend listens to you when you need it most, not just when it's convenient.

Parents may get impatient when their kids talk on the phone all day to their friends, but it's hard to imagine teenage life without that. In societies where there aren't many telephones, teens still gather around the village fountain or in the corner of the market-place to talk and talk and talk. It's as if our souls want to share everything when we are young. But what about listening? I'm sure you have friends you like very much who would rather talk than listen. But when you really feel sad or troubled, it's your turn to talk and theirs to listen. Will they? Can you count on it?

By *listening* I mean really taking in what you have to say. If I say to a friend, "I'm scared that I've done something wrong," or, "I'm facing a tough decision and I just don't know what to do," I don't want him to reply with, "Don't worry about it," or, "Let's get a pizza. You'll be okay."

I want him to listen.

I want to know that he understands and cares about my situation. That's how true friends react. They don't try to change the subject quickly. They don't bring the conversation back to themselves. I know that one of the hardest things in the world is to talk about what's really bothering you. This isn't restricted to teens. Only the youngest children—and the most honest adults—can find the courage to show that they have doubts and fears deep down. But we all do, and when the time comes to speak out your secret worries, you want someone there who will accept what you have to say. Even if it makes him squirm. Even if it makes you squirm. When the talk is over and you have brought your hidden worry out into the open, you will know if you have been listened to, because you and your friend will feel closer than ever. And if you are fortunate and your friend really takes your feelings to heart, you will find that a little bit of your burden has been lifted.

Just because someone listened.

2. A true friend feels happy for the good things in your life, even when she doesn't get anything for herself.

Maybe this is a subtle point, but I've put it high on the list. A true friend knows how to be happy for you. When you get an A on a test or make the varsity team, her eyes shine with as much joy as yours. She doesn't feel secretly jealous. She doesn't envy your happiness and wish it belonged to her instead. Your happiness *is* hers.

The reason I put this quality high on the list is that after years of observing people, I think being happy for others is a rare gift. Not as rare as an extinct animal, but rare enough. This quality is called empathy, which is like sympathy—they share the same root word—but sympathy carries a sad association. We send sympathy cards when someone dies or gets sick. Empathy is both positive and negative. It means you are open to how others feel. People who have empathy are never alone, because in their heart they know how to bond with other people. Empathy means you never shut anyone out. You aren't afraid of people just because you can feel them.

In fact, you *want* to feel them.

See why I call this a rare gift? Do you want to feel how sad it is for someone to lose a parent in a divorce? To feel someone who has come in last in a race or has run out of money? These are tough things to feel. But unless you can feel other people, you will not be able to have one of the greatest joys in life, which is to bond. When you and a friend bond, it's like having someone inside your heart. You are so close you almost breathe the same breath—at least when you have those special close moments.

Sharing tears and laughter is what a true friend is about. And just because it is difficult to feel someone else's happiness when they won the race but you didn't, when they got the A and you got the C, I treasure any friend who feels that close to me.

So close that my happiness is automatically theirs.

3. A true friend tells you the truth when it counts.

What if the worst thing someone told you was the truth? Would you walk away from him? Most people would. So having a friend you can be really honest with is a gift. Truth has a lot of enemies, and not all of them are lies. Early on in the game I'm sure you learned one of the tricks of making friends with someone: flattery. "Oh, you are so beautiful today. I can't wait to see those clothes on you. Everything you do is so cool." Flattery isn't like lying. You don't exactly say what's false. You just learn to pick out the things that will please the other person the most. But flattery isn't the same as telling the truth, either.

Why? Because you are being selective. You are leaving out all the unpleasant things, like picking through a box of chocolates for the best creams and leaving behind the rest. If you have to flatter someone to be friends with him, I doubt that you have a true friend. In fact, I can almost be sure of it. And if someone is always playing up to you, trying to make you think you're wonderful all the time, I wouldn't be sure that he can tell you the truth when you need to hear it.

What kinds of things does a true friend tell you when it counts? I'm not thinking of negative things. You don't need someone to tell you that you're not good enough or that people don't like you or that your dreams are foolish and will never come true. Those sorts of negative opinions never help anyone. The truth helps. That's how I would judge what I need to hear. Does it help me to see something I couldn't see for myself? Imagine your best friend saying any of the following things to you:

"You're giving up. Keep going."

"You need me to help you, and I'm not going away until you let me."

"You're hurting somebody else, and it has to stop."

"You're too full of yourself."

"That's just self-pity talking. Be brave."

These are the kinds of sentences we all have to hear at one time or another. They sting. They aren't what we like to tell ourselves. They don't make us feel terrific when we hear them. But if they come from a true friend, they are often the truth. Not that the truth has to be negative. A true friend also knows when to say "You're great" and "I love you, man" just when it helps you to hear those things. Our souls want us to live the truth, and they are constantly sending us signals so that we can find the truth for ourselves. That's mostly what spiritual life is about. But when your soul isn't getting the message across to you, it's your true friends who step in and do it for you.

4. A true friend accepts who you are without judging you.

I just said that I want a true friend to tell me the truth. But I don't want her to put me down. In our heart of hearts we all have less than wonderful thoughts about other people. That includes the people we call our friends. *He's too fat. She's not as pretty as she thinks she is. He tries to be cool, but it comes off as cocky.* When you have these negative opinions, they are called judgments. A judgment isn't just any negative thought. It's a thought that makes another person wrong or guilty or shameful. Strangely, many people think they are being helpful by voicing their negative judgments.

Consider the following examples.

Bad-mouthing in Disguise: "Helpful" Advice That Really Hurts

"You need to work on that body of yours."

"There you go, saying all the wrong things."

"That girl/boy will never go out with someone like you."

"I heard something really mean about you."

"Some kids are saying you're not cool."

"Don't be so stupid next time."

"You're better off keeping your mouth shut."

"I would never do that. What were you thinking?"

Let me be very clear. If I had a friend who said these things, even jokingly, more than a few times, we would stop being friends pretty fast. And I don't say these things to my friends either. If you're in doubt about the advice you want to give, just apply the same opinion to yourself and imagine how you'd feel.

Does it make you feel bad about yourself that you're not pretty or that you're fat or that some kids talk about you behind your back? No question. So you don't need to deliver that news to anybody.

Do you already feel afraid that you might say the wrong thing or look dumb? Of course. So you don't need to call anybody else out on that score.

Would it make you feel ashamed if someone called you stupid, uncool, a bad person, a slut? I don't have to answer that one. You already know you're not doing anyone a favor by repeating such things.

These are all harsh judgments, and yet teens blurt them out all the time. It's one of the most regrettable aspects of peer pressure that we try to belong by running others down. We try to feel big by making them look small. It never works, and yet because judging others is the easy way out, many people learn this bad habit in adolescence and keep it up as adults.

A true friend doesn't judge. If you are fat, your friend accepts you. Not in spite of the fact that you are fat. Not overlooking that you are fat. Not hiding the truth in her heart that she thinks fat is disgusting. Anyone can do those things, telling you, "Oh, you're not really that fat. Everyone loves you anyway. Have another ice cream sundae. You'll feel better." That's not what a true friend does. A true friend loves you from the soul level, and at that level none of us are victims of our worst qualities. What hurts so much about being judged is that secretly—or not so secretly—you believe the bad things that are being said. You feel ugly or dumb or ashamed. Your soul exists to tell you that these judgments aren't true. Period. They are things you've gotten stuck in your mind like stubborn bacteria. Each and every day your soul is trying to find ways to defeat these nasty bugs that attack the truth, which is that you are totally good and beautiful, totally worthy to be loved. On your soul journey you will discover just how totally wrong your judgments have been.

Take a true friend with you on this journey. You have a lot of truth and a lot of joy to share along the way.

5. A true friend is someone you can tell a secret to without being afraid he will spread it around.

Gossip is a funny thing. We all know it's wrong, but we all do it. The best gossip, of course, is when you know a secret about someone. Then you get the thrill of telling everyone else, and for that little moment when you are in prize possession of a naughty secret, just itching to spread it around, the imp of gossip has you in its power. It's about to make you do something malicious, and even though you may live to regret it, you can't help but give in.

Gossip isn't going away because it's wrong. But at least my true friend won't gossip about me. He won't take a secret that I had the courage to share and spread it around like free five-dollar bills. He won't make me the butt of laughter. He won't have fun at my expense. I think gossip is usually just a sign of how bored some people are with their life. In that sense it's harmless enough. But at the soul level it's not so harmless. We hurt another person's spirit when we ridicule them or betray their feelings.

Even when they aren't there to hear us.

That's the thing most of us don't realize. Talking behind someone else's back has the same power to hurt as doing it to their face. But the hurt is more invisible. It happens at the spiritual level. When you ridicule someone to their face, you can immediately see the hurt you've caused. But just think of somebody at school who everyone agrees is a loser. They laugh at her expense behind her back. They think it's really funny when she messes up one more time. When you see her in the hall, doesn't that girl avoid your gaze or hang her head or shoot you a look that says, *I know what you're saying about me*? That's because she does know. At the spiritual level we all know who is on our side and who has set their judgment against us. We know when we've been hurt, even when we weren't there to see it.

So, hard as it is to resist juicy gossip, a true friend just does. No matter what. And if he slips and betrays what I have told him in secret, he is brave enough to come to me and confess what he did. He knows I won't be happy. He knows that our friendship has been wounded for a while. But it would be a worse wound to hurt me behind my back and not tell me.

6. A true friend loves you even though you aren't perfect.

"I'm not perfect, but I'm getting better." I can't remember where I first heard that saying, but it's a fine one to live by. Nobody expects you to be perfect, because it's impossible in the first place and very hard work in the second place. Yet the desire to be perfect isn't easy to give up. Some inner voice tells us we have to be perfect or we aren't any good at all. If you have never heard this voice, I'm glad, because many if not most young people do. Where does this voice come from? It comes from other people who expect a lot from you. Parents and teachers, to begin with. They apply pressure for you to succeed, and because you are afraid to let them down, the inner voice starts saying, "You can't fail one little bit. If you do, nobody's going to like you anymore. You have to be perfect."

I want one true friend who doesn't look at me this way—not at all. This friend loves me even when I fall flat on my face. She expects me to do my best, and that is good enough. Being perfect isn't the same as being happy. When people hear this, they often don't believe it. They think that being perfect, like being rich, has to equate with happiness. After all, that's their whole motivation. Being perfect or rich—how wonderful if you can be both!—stands for the ideal life.

A true friend is there to give you a little kick in the pants if you start thinking that way. Because perfection has this nasty little habit of becoming an addiction. Don't you know girls who obsess about being the perfect weight? We all do, at every stage

of life. It's pretty easy to see that in time they will want the perfect boyfriend, followed by the perfect college, the perfect job, the perfect husband, and, to crown everything, perfect children. What they don't see is that those children will feel miserable because so much pressure will be put on them. Perfect is impossible except at the soul level, and there it isn't a matter of weight, boyfriends, jobs, husbands, or anything else in the outside world.

Perfect at the soul level is perfect love. It's perfect truth. It's perfect attunement with the universe. These are inner pefections, not outer ones. Every day your soul wants you to come closer and closer to achieving that kind of perfection. It's the only kind that never brings misery or stress or pressure from other people. All inner perfection can bring is increased joy and a more expanded life. I want a friend who can expand with me, who knows me from the inside and loves me from there.

7. A true friend inspires you.

I know it can be tough to hang around someone who is better than you at a lot of things. But instead of making it a competition, look at it another way. Be inspired by your friend without comparing yourself with him. Inspiration is a quality of the soul. The two words *spirit* and *inspire* come from the same root word, in fact. When you are inspired by someone, you share in his spirit, and at the same time you feed your own spirit.

So find someone to look up to and become friends. You don't have to flatter him or tell him how great he is. But do say what you find inspiring about him. Certainly that will attract his interest, because we all like to be told how good we are. Sincere admiration is a great foundation for a friendship. And often you will find that the person who inspires you has another surprising trait: He will admire you in return. A true friend respects you and never uses you as a foil to make himself look better. It doesn't matter that you might not be as pretty, smart, rich, or talented. Still your friend sees something special in you—and that is inspiring in and of itself.

8. A true friend doesn't care what others say about you.

Sometimes a friend has to be stronger than you are. It's almost impossible to be independent of what others think. When you hear that other kids are talking about you, even when you are afraid it's bad, you still want to hear. Most of the time what they are saying isn't good for your self-esteem. Gossip is about running people down behind their back. But at least your true friend can love you despite what anybody says. In your teenage years it's hard to believe, but the in crowd at school aren't the ones who are going to be the most happy and successful in life. Usually they are the ones most attached to looking good and impressing everyone with their coolness.

But what's really behind this desire to be in? Think about it. Aren't these the very people who care the most about what others are thinking? If they didn't, they wouldn't have to try so hard. The in crowd also exists to reject those who don't fit in. They judge and put down other kids for no good reason except that making someone else feel small or inferior makes them feel secure. Don't be fooled: There is no security in your life when you depend upon making others look small. You will always be resented, even if on the surface people pretend to admire you.

A true friend keeps your head on straight about these things. She can say, "Cool isn't everything. If they knew you the way I do, nobody would ever run you down." And these words will be sincere, because if a friend is close enough to your soul, she can see how trivial all the social stuff really is. Have at least one friend who can see you through the eyes of the soul, and you will be protected—as best as anyone can be—from the social cruelty that plays such a huge part in this time of life you are passing through.

9. A true friend respects you.

There are lots of reasons why kids are afraid to ask for respect. First, it's something adults are always demanding in one way or another. "As long as you're in my house, you will respect my rules." Who hasn't heard these words from an angry father at least once? Maybe a lot more than once. Adults talk about how respect must be earned, which sounds intimidating. It can sound as if you have to win a baseball game single-handedly, or save a baby from a burning house, before anyone will respect you.

But respect is another quality of the soul. I would call it the "equality" of the soul, because for me to respect you, you don't really have to do anything but show me your soul. Behind all the masks each of us is equal and deserves equal respect. If you can find a friend who knows this, you have found a treasure.

Because kids don't expect anyone to respect them, they often fall into behavior where they don't respect one another, either. You are disrespecting someone, even when you don't mean to, by exhibiting the following behavior:

Making fun of them when they are doing their best

Pointing out their flaws

Showing off that you have more money and nicer things

Running down their parents or their brothers and sisters

Criticizing their faith

Treating them as if their feelings don't matter

School is full of this kind of behavior, and I think the reason is what I've just mentioned: You can't give respect when you are afraid to ask for it. Each of us might pretend that it's okay to hear someone rag on our little brother or boast that their father makes more money. We wince inside but pretend not to when someone laughs at how badly we caught a football or missed an easy pitch playing baseball. The right thing to do is not to pretend. When someone shows you disrespect, you don't have to call them on it. But don't keep pretending it didn't happen. Either go up to them afterward and quietly point out what happened, or if that isn't possible, be on the lookout for those true friends who really do respect you. They are the ones who don't laugh at your weakness and never boast about money.

I'm sure you get the point, but there's another thing I'd like to mention. Sometimes when you disagree with someone or call them out for good reason, they will turn on you and say, "You're disrespecting me." Actually, when you know you're in the right, it's a mark of character to stand up for what you think, even if you have to disagree with somebody. It takes even more character when that somebody is a friend. Don't let the word *disrespect* scare you off. True respect isn't about opinions. It's not about who is right or wrong. It's about equality of the soul. If you can keep that in mind, you will earn people's respect and find it much easier to give respect in return.

10. A true friend lives in your heart like a part of yourself.

I left this quality for last even though you might think it should come first. I left it for last because this is one thing that can creep up on you. The people who really live in our heart are not always easy to notice. We take them for granted because they are always there. I hope you have the wonderful experience of being able to take many people into your heart. It's a rare ability because most people think that it's just your family who should be given such a place. Or perhaps the person you fall in love with romantically.

I think the heart is much bigger than that. It can include anyone whose soul feels especially close. You find yourself feeling the way she feels, thinking the way she thinks. You can share silent moments without having to talk too much. And above all, you are never afraid or insecure around such a person. I'd call these the touchstones, the telltale signs. For you'll find that there will be those you fall in love with who make you feel insecure and not very safe. That's one of the peculiar things about romance, that it can make you afraid because you feel so open and vulnerable.

Sometimes this changes, and those you love turn out to find a place in your heart. But mostly, I find, it's the true friends who get there first and stay there. Girls are supposed to be better at this than boys. Not because boys don't have big hearts, but other things get in the way. Trying to look cool or act tough. Trying to be a winner. Trying to make others think you're better than you are or turning every encounter into a competition. Boys are like that quite a lot of the time. Even so, the soul doesn't care if you are a boy or a girl. It naturally wants to be close to other souls, and if you let it do what it wants, there is no limit to the number of people who can live in your heart. Be on the lookout. You'll be surprised who might belong in there after all.

Soul Mates

Q: Do I have a soul mate? When will I meet him?

A: I sat down to answer this question when I noticed that it came from a thirteen-year-old girl. I paused, trying not to be shocked. Why was someone that young thinking about a soul mate already? But I quickly realized that the phrase *soul mate* has become part of romantic lore, like Prince Charming. I have a soft feeling for romantic lore. I hope and believe that I am my wife's Prince Charming. But if you are asking me about the one and only love who is perfectly matched to you and has traveled across the universe to find you, I don't believe in waiting for such a phenomenon.

It's a great achievement for any person to make a good match that allows both partners to grow. You can start now with someone you really like and feel close to. It's less romantic than sitting in your tower until the day a hero sweeps you off your feet, but in truth, if you relate to everyone as an equal soul, you will also be better off when it comes time to pick that special person who will be your mate.

Anyway, aren't all souls a perfect match if you come right down to it?

Falling in Love

Q: I have crushes all the time. Is this okay? What is the spiritual side of falling in love?

A: The heart is a muscle, and like all muscles, it needs exercise. Crushes are a way for the heart to feel bursts of intense joy, pain, fear, and wonder all at the same time. That's a kind of exercise, not physically, but emotionally. I would rather have too many crushes than none at all.

As for the spiritual side of falling in love, I must confess that to me, falling in love is spiritual all by itself. What's it like to fall in love? You change, and everything around you changes. The ordinary world lights up. You feel that you are walking on air. The person you love is perfect in every way. The future will be just as perfect once you two are together forever.

These perceptions don't last, yet I think they give us a glimpse into how the soul really feels. At the soul level there is lightness and love that changes the world. You aren't bound by fences on all sides, but are free. You can be what you want to be and do what you want to do. That feeling of power and freedom comes with falling in love.

Only, you have to turn fantasy into reality. The only problem with falling in love is that it often turns out to be too much fantasy and not enough reality. The reality of the soul is waiting for you once you go on the spiritual journey. Let your crushes be what they are: a little taste of the soul's reality.

Falling Out of Love

Q: I am eighteen and almost married someone I deeply loved. At the last minute I listened to my parents, and after a few months my "true love" and I split up after I found out he was seeing another girl. I am hurt and bitter. What is falling out of love all about?

A: I wish this were an easier question, because falling out of love doesn't just hurt. It often brings disillusionment. When you fall in love, everything feels wonderful and perfect. There is a kind of shield that protects you from ordinary worries and disappointments. When you fall out of love, the shield drops. Even though you are only returning to ordinary life, the experience feels bigger. You feel as if you almost touched perfection, only to lose it again.

I don't think that feeling should be trusted. Falling in love isn't an illusion, but it's not necessarily meant to last. As I mentioned above, this is a glimpse at the soul's reality. As you fall out of love, that glimpse vanishes, but it was still real, you still felt it and got to experience what it was like. So don't be bitter and fight against disillusionment. Nothing wrong has happened to you. Love is a cosmic force. Its glory awaits you and can never be lost. As you nurse your hurt feelings, keep your eyes on a future in which love blossoms again.

God

"DOES GOD REALLY EXIST? HOW CAN I BE SURE?"

People fight over God. They always have, and it keeps on going. Here we are in so-called modern times, but the same ancient argument is still raging: *My God is better than your God. If you don't believe in mine, you must die.* Someone once calculated that every year sees thirty wars around the world. Most are wars started about God, and even when they aren't, the two enemies boast, "God is on our side."

It's tragic enough that people fight over God, given that God is supposed to be about love and forgiveness, about living together and being part of one family. But here's an even stranger thing: Everyone seems to be getting worked up over somebody they've never even met. God is invisible. He once walked in the Garden of Eden, according to the Book of Genesis, but that was because he wanted to admire the Paradise he had just created. Now he lives, well, somewhere else. Perhaps in heaven, perhaps in some home that is beyond time and space.

FACE-TO-FACE WITH GOD

Wouldn't it be nice to actually meet God before starting a fight over him? In fact, wouldn't it be right to meet God before having any strong opinion about her? (Don't get too comfortable calling God a he, since being part of everything, God is just as easily wor-

shipped as a she. I'll keep using *he* only because that's been the usual way for hundreds of years.)

I know it's too much to ask people to stop fighting over God right this minute. But you and everyone you know can still hope to meet God. Does that sound impossible? In fact, God can be met in many ways that are everyday experiences.

How Do I Meet God?

He can be met in his creation.

He can be met in your heart.

He can be met in your mind.

He can be met in love for other people.

He can be met in your being.

If you begin to notice each encounter you have with God, over time you will meet God more often and more deeply. One day you will have a truly close encounter, one that will change your life.

It all begins by being awake to those small moments when spirit is close, because spirit is God. Get yourself a blank notebook or diary. This is what you'll use to record all your encounters. You might want to title it "Close Encounters" or "My Time with God."

Now, for the next thirty days be on the lookout for anything that fits the list I just gave.

Meeting God in His Creation
Examples
"Today I saw a beautiful sunset that took my breath away. I was out walking and my eyes soared up to a towering white cloud—it was glorious."

"This evening I walked out and looked at the stars. My mind was filled with wonder to think about them and the infinity that lies beyond the stars."

Meeting God in Your Heart
Examples
"Today I was alone and felt really at peace. The world is okay and so am I."

"I was in the woods today and felt that I was totally one with nature—I wish I could feel that every day."

"I began to feel that I might be able to love a higher power, just because I am so grateful for being here."

Meeting God in Your Mind
Examples
"Today I looked at a rose, and it was so incredibly beautiful I wanted to know what kind of mind could create such a thing."

"I thought of somebody's name and the next minute they called me on the phone—I felt a shiver, as if the universe had read my mind."

"I closed my eyes and tried to imagine infinity. I didn't get there, but I almost felt I touched it."

Meeting God in Love for Other People
Examples

"I was amazed today at how much I love _____."

"I think he/she is a beautiful soul."

"I noticed today that when someone is asleep, no matter who they are, they look pure, for just a moment like an angel."

"I saw a stranger on the street, and all at once I felt I could love that person if we knew each other."

Meeting God in Your Being
Examples

"Today for just a moment I realized that I belong and my life matters. I saw my uniqueness."

"Today I felt that my life is a privilege to live. I could be really exceptional in some way."

"Today felt like the best time to be alive."

These are just a few samples to get you started. Notice that none of them use the word *God*. You don't have to; you only have to be personal and true to your feelings. That isn't always easy. Boys in particular might not feel comfortable if their buddies thought they were writing down sissy things about glorious clouds and loving life. But we all have these moments, and this diary of your close encounters with spirit is just for you. I can promise you that if you actually give this experiment a chance, your spirit will open up amazingly in thirty days—you won't be the same person. Your appreciation of your own existence will begin to blossom, and once it's started, there is no end to that process.

Now we're going to take the radical step of inviting God to return to Earth and not stay so far away. There's no Garden of Eden for him to walk in, but my approach isn't religious anyway. We've already touched on the need to be spiritual without feeling that you have to obey a certain religion and follow its beliefs to the letter. If you respect every religion, you have taken a step toward peace. I think God loves peace more than any other quality of spirit, so that's a really good start. We're off to actually find God by searching for him at the soul level—the biggest treasure hunt ever conceived and the only trip that deserves to be called cosmic.

So let's get right down to it.

Looking for God

Q: I know that some people spend all their life trying to find God. How does that work? Do I just pray and wait?

A: It's more than prayer and it's more than waiting. First you have to decide whether God is outside yourself. A God who is outside yourself would be different from one who is inside. Of course, we all have been taught that it's a little of both. When you read poetry like

God's in his heaven—
All's right with the world

almost automatically you see an image of a person, "God," living in a place, "heaven," that isn't inside you. When people pray, they send their prayers to God, so again it's almost automatic to think of your prayer being like a letter you send in the mail.

Yet when you think about feeling God's love, that feeling must occur inside you. The same goes for God's peace and comfort. So should you look for God both inside and outside? For thousands of years people have done both. In fact, just as you go somewhere on summer vacation, the faithful once spent vast amounts of money and time to go to sacred places where God supposedly lived (in some parts of the world they still do). Pilgrims sought out holy temples or places of ancient power that were said to be special to God. Once they got there, they expected an inner experience that would validate that God's presence was actually to be found at the end of the trail.

GOD IS A JOURNEY

You can seek God in this way if you wish. But I think the inward journey to find God is the same as the outward journey, and it doesn't require you to leave home. The inward journey is the same as seeking your soul. In other words, you are really seeking a part of yourself. But unlike your hand, which you don't have to seek because it's just there in plain sight, or your mind, which you don't have to seek because you have thoughts all the time, your soul lies beyond. Beyond what? Beyond the everyday activity of the world. If you are going to find God, you have to find a way to see past all the things that life throws at you day in and day out. Here's how to do that.

LEARNING FROM THE RIVER

Imagine that your life is like a river flowing very fast on the surface. That would stand for all the actions that take up your time every day. From the moment you first open your eyes in the morning, you greet a world full of sights and sounds. Other people want you to do all kinds of things. Your mind jumps into all this activity and rushes along with it.

But just beneath the surface a river runs quieter and more slowly. You are like that too. Beneath all the jumble of activity your mind is not so active. I'm sure you've noticed this, although maybe you haven't paid all that much attention to what lies beneath the surface. You may not have noticed, for example, those moments of peace that come when you are lying on your back in the grass just staring at clouds, or when you drowsily begin to fall asleep, or when you are suddenly struck by how beautiful a sunset is. But the mind does pause for a second and experience a bit more stillness then.

At the very bottom a river flows very, very slowly. You are like that also, because if you go inward seeking God, you can learn to dive into the silence and total stillness of your mind. Now you are truly going beyond. You are taking seriously the great saying "Be still, and know that I am God." What is at the

very bottom of a river? Bedrock, the support that holds the whole river together. The bedrock doesn't flow at all, yet without it the river wouldn't exist.

Likewise, to find God, you must dive down to the bedrock of your own self. There, at the source, you will discover something amazing. As you encounter your own soul, God will show up in the outer world. Your five senses will wake up to a presence that is behind everything, and that presence is alive, intelligent, and full of love.

But What Do I Do?

Q: I can understand your image of the river, but in practical terms what do I do?

A: If you think about it, there are only four things you can do:

> You can think.

> You can feel.

> You can act.

> You can be.

These four things aren't special or exotic. You do them every moment of the day. If I had a video camera mounted on your shoulder to follow you from the moment you woke up to the moment you went to bed, it would discover you either thinking, feeling, acting, or being. You can't escape these basic aspects of being alive. (We're assuming here that the video camera is special and can look inside to watch you think.) Finding God turns on these four things. So the tools you need have always been part of your life.

TURNING YOUR THOUGHTS TOWARD GOD

There are lots of ways to do this. You can read about God in scriptures and other writings devoted to God. You can set a few moments aside to contemplate God. You can pray. All of these are valid ways that people have used to turn their thoughts away from the outside world, directing them toward the world of God. The two are the same world, but you are putting your attention on the finer aspects of creation. If you play baseball after school, your thoughts will be on the game, but you might look up while standing in the outfield and notice how beautiful the evening sky is. That's a finer aspect of creation. These finer aspects are everywhere, waiting to be noticed. And although this may sound strange, when you notice them, they notice you back. There's an intelligence that looks back at us when we look in its direction. When you begin to sense this silent observer, your mind is beginning to notice God.

TURNING YOUR FEELINGS TOWARD GOD

Just as you have finer thoughts, you also have finer feelings. For example, when you want to stay on the phone and talk to your friends, but your mother wants you to get off the phone and do your schoolwork, what do you feel? Irritated, impatient, put upon. Maybe a little stressed or frustrated. Those are typical feelings when we don't get to do what we want to do. But at other moments you might stop to notice how much love there is in your mother's eyes or how peaceful she looks. Those are finer feelings. All they require is paying attention. You can walk past a garden without noticing it, or you can stop and really look. When you really look, your feelings shift. *Ah, it's beautiful.* The same thing often happens looking at photographs of people from around the world. Someone who has no meaning to you except as a stranger or a foreigner (perhaps, alas, even an enemy) turns out to be just like you. A look in the eyes captures your attention, and suddenly you have a finer feeling. If you keep noticing these finer feelings, you will discover a layer of emotion inside yourself that doesn't care about differences. You begin to experience love for all of life, a reverence for creation, and a special feeling of belonging. In this way your emotions have turned toward God.

TURNING YOUR ACTIONS TOWARD GOD

We all know that there are good actions and bad actions, selfish actions and altruistic actions. For a long, long time people have felt that good actions are closer to God, along with selfless or altruistic actions. Children are taught that it is better to give than to receive. They are taught to do volunteer work and to help those less fortunate than themselves. But in my mind action goes further than that. To really turn your action toward God, you have to complete a circle, and here's what I mean by that.

If someone surprises you with a small gift you weren't expecting, you can mutter a small, embarrassed thanks and walk away. Or you can return that gift with real thanks from your heart, meeting the person's eyes and letting them see that you were really touched. The first reaction breaks the circle, the second reaction completes the circle. That's one example. You can find yourself getting a little extra money. What do you do with it? You can hoard it away, intending to spend it all on yourself. Or you could give a bit of money to someone who has less. The first action breaks the circle, the second completes it. This second example may not seem so clear, however. What kind of circle are you completing by giving money to someone less fortunate?

Here the second action is returning something to the source. Any time you give, you are saying, "I know this money came from God, and in thanks I am returning some of it to the source." It doesn't have to be money—you can return a kind gesture, a favor, a compliment. Anything, really. Everything that comes your way must have a source. I'm not saying you have to call this source God. You could be saying, "Everything comes from the universe and goes back to it. I want to show that I understand this." Whatever words you use, you are acknowledging that there is a source that gives, and when you give back, you are closing the circle of creation. Being kind to a young child closes the circle because you are showing reverence to the time when you were a child. Being kind to older people shows reverence to the old age that will one day greet you. When your actions close the circle, you have turned them toward God.

TURNING YOUR BEING TOWARD GOD

To be is simple but deep. It's simple because everyone exists. You don't have to do anything to be. You don't have to feel anything to be. You don't have to think anything to be. You just are. But existence is also deep. What makes it deep? Your being is connected to awareness. Unlike a rock, which just sits there, you can say, "I am." There's no simpler phrase in any language, and yet *I am* contains a lot. It contains a sense of belonging. It contains a sense that you are where you should be. It contains a sense of alertness and observation. *I am* is your connection to life itself.

Some of these things may sound foreign to how you are living right now, but I imagine that quite a few sound familiar. Some teens are already very alert. They look around with eagerness; they rush into the unknown, wanting to find everything there is to find. Other teens (like people in general) are sleepier, dull, not curious. They rarely observe anything new. This isn't a criticism;

I just want to give you a very clear choice of how to participate. You can be as alert and alive as possible, or you can sleepwalk your way through the whole thing. I'm not saying that your choice is to worship God or not. Just think back on that comment from Einstein, that there are only two ways to live: Either nothing is a miracle, or everything is a miracle. When you live as if everything is a miracle, you have turned your being toward God.

Where Is God?

Q: **Where does God live? I mean, if he lives in heaven, where is that located, somewhere in the sky?**

A: God can't have an ordinary home with an address, even in the sky, because he is everywhere. If everywhere is his address, that changes a lot of how we think about him. Imagine yourself about to get into a fight. Just as you are about to unleash some nasty words or cock back your fist, your mind says, *God is everywhere. He is even in this guy I am about to fight with.* That would be strange, wouldn't it? What if you were watching TV and the news showed a convict being led off to prison? There he is in his orange jumpsuit, head hanging down and wrists handcuffed behind his back. Suddenly your mind says, *God is everywhere. He is in this abject criminal.* That would be strange too.

Because the minute you really take seriously that God is everywhere, something happens. You can't pretend he is somewhere else. In other words, you can't say, "I hate this guy I'm about to fight with, so God isn't in him." You can't say, "That criminal robbed somebody, so God isn't in him." None of us has the ability to say where God is and where he isn't. The truth is that God, being cosmic, *has* to be everywhere. He has no choice, and neither do we.

It makes you think, doesn't it? If each person paused for even five minutes a day to think this one thought—*God is everywhere*—ordinary life would never be the same again. If you want to go deeply into it, here's the next question that pops up:

Where is everywhere?

LOOKING EVERYWHERE FOR GOD

First, there's the everywhere you can't see. It is invisible and totally beyond the five senses. This is because it's not part of physical creation. The strongest radio telescope looking to the farthest reaches of the universe would never be able to locate this place. It has no physical existence, even as a faint vibration. It uses no energy at all. Therefore, it has been called pure being, because it exists without using matter or energy. The phrase *pure potential* can also be used for this aspect of God. It's the ability to create before anything is actually created. This may sound strange, but refer back to yourself. You have the ability to create sentences even when you aren't saying anything. God is that same potential—silent and unseen—on an infinite scale.

That's the first way of thinking about where God is.

Second, there's the everywhere that is *almost* in the physical world, just shy of being seen. This location, which sounds a bit like a ghost, has been called the subtle world. It's the world of images, thoughts, and inspiration. But also located here are myths and dreams and wishes. The seeds of the future are planted here.

When we say that someone has a vision of possibilities, the subtle world is the source of the vision. For many centuries the subtle world has been considered the home of God and the angels (also the devil and his demons). To me it is the zone of miracles, a place where physical boundaries disappear and rules of existence can be bent. When you hear about God sitting on his throne in heaven, that image comes from the subtle world.

That's the second way of thinking about where God is.

Third, there's the everywhere you are familiar with already, the infinite expanse of the universe. Here the five senses bring us all our information, and even though God cannot be seen, what we can observe is the incredible order and beauty of creation. That orderliness implies a creator. Therefore, it's just as accurate to say that God exists here as it is to say he exists in heaven or in the realm of pure being.

That's the third way of thinking about where God is.

Everywhere has three locations, and so does God. Of course, what would be even more fascinating is the possibility that you might also be living in all three places. I think you are. You don't have to wait to go to heaven to realize that you are already living with God, in the exact place where he is. Or rather, the exact three places.

How Do You Know?

Q: How do you personally know that God is real?

A: As a doctor, I have a background in science. I learned something that holds true in any field of science, which is that nature is more powerful at the invisible level. It took medicine more than two thousand years to discover that invisible organisms called germs could create disease—before that, it was possible to believe that illness was carried into a house on the wind (the word *malaria* comes from the Italian for "bad air," as if this disease were actually caused by a certain kind of air).

GOD'S INVISIBLE WORLD

To get even more basic, you can't see an atom through a microscope, yet a tremendous amount of power is contained in a single atom. I also learned that nature is organized from an invisible level. You can't see what holds your body together, yet if some invisible force did not, your cells would fly apart into space as a cloud of energy.

I come from India, where this invisible region has been pondered for thousands of years, an amazing thing when you consider that there were no microscopes. Nevertheless, the ancient sages and teachers wanted to know what existed beyond the visible world. Who was it that controlled all this power and organization? The ancient ones were like detectives into the invisible. How do you become a detective when you can't even see your clues? You go inside yourself. After all, you can't see a thought or a feeling, but you know that these are real.

The ancient ones went even deeper than thought. They decided that if you can see God, you haven't found him yet. If you can think about God, you haven't found him yet. If you can imagine God, you haven't found him yet. (See what an amazing journey this must have been? Because most people are satisfied to think about God and imagine what he must be like.)

Eventually what they found was the invisible region inside themselves. And there was God, not as a person or a feeling or a thought, but as power itself, creativity itself, reality itself. This is hard to understand unless you go on the journey personally—which I hope you will do. That's what this book has been all about, looking beyond the surface of life to find the infinite power and intelligence that lies beyond. You don't have to finish the whole journey to find God. The ancient ones, who spent generations on their detective hunt, didn't find all of God themselves.

But they discovered what God is made of, and you can too. By understanding what science already knows, and by taking a spiritual journey into yourself, you can prove that God exists personally. The version of God that you find will be your own. Nobody else has to agree. You be the detective and follow your own clues.

Needing God

Q: I have a friend who got very sick. I prayed for him every day, but he isn't better. This makes me wonder: Who needs God if he doesn't answer our prayers?

A: Let me thank you for the honesty of your question. Deep down we all get disappointed when our prayers aren't answered. We are told that God works in mysterious ways, but once you feel let down, it's easy to begin to lose faith in God.

But I don't believe in a God who is real only if he brings me what I want. After all, God isn't supposed to be a vending machine that grants wishes every time I slip in a prayer. God exists to fulfill needs that no one can fulfill in any other way. Here are just a few.

TO INSPIRE YOU

What inspires you? I mean really deep down. A painting that is so powerful you could cry or laugh for joy just looking at it? Maybe music works that way for you, or a person who has touched your heart. Life would be unbearably dull and flat if we didn't, each in our own way, look for inspiration. In every part of the world the most beautiful objects created by man were made to praise God. If you travel to Europe and stand in front of a French cathedral, you are seeing a monument to God that took hundreds of people to build. Often three generations would devote their entire working lives to the project.

Many times in building a cathedral disaster would strike.

Roofs collapsed, killing everyone underneath. Fires broke out and destroyed decades of work. The plague might wipe out half the workers in one summer. But nothing could stop a whole town from erecting a shrine to faith. Their purpose wasn't to obtain money or success, but to build a house worthy of God's majesty, which was the same purpose, thousands of years before, behind building the Great Pyramid at Giza in Egypt, the largest man-made structure on Earth for more than three thousand years. In both cases a whole society was inspired by an idea. Call the idea eternity or infinity or almighty power, it was part of how they saw God.

Now, you aren't called upon to build a cathedral, probably not even a church, but God inspires more than art. He inspires people to be good, to rise above themselves, to look upon other human beings as equals. You can be inspired by your own spirit. Just ask yourself, "What am I inspired to do?" You will get a feeling close to your heart. It will lead you to something a lot more beautiful than you ever thought you could achieve: singing from your heart, painting a picture that expresses who you are, writing a poem, reaching out in kindness. But you could also be inspired to make the varsity team or invent a new dessert. Any inspiration is an inspiration from God in the end. God and spirit are the same, and both want one thing only: expansion of your heart so that you feel the joy of life.

TO BRING INNER PEACE

The need for inner peace is greater than ever. A generation ago I doubt I would have been talking to a young person about inner peace. Things have changed, however, to bring much more stress at a younger age, so that even grade school kids worry about the world and their future in it.

What do you do when you are really worried? You can try to escape, but without peace your worries and stress return very quickly. It's like running into a movie house to get out of the rain, only to discover that the rain hasn't stopped when the movie is over. The same is true of your inner storms. The only solution is to find a place inside yourself that is always peaceful.

This is the peace of the soul. If you have ever learned about meditation, you know that it's a way of finding one's inner peace. I've started lots of teens meditating, and they often say it's not easy at first: "Wow, I never knew it was so noisy in my head." "I felt so jumpy I could hardly keep my eyes open." "I could feel all these thoughts buzzing around my head." These are typical comments at first. But without exception, each person eventually found the place of peace that is inside everyone. Once they did, they really liked it. The comments changed: "I touched the silence." "I felt something really special I've never felt before—I was totally relaxed." "I closed my eyes and twenty minutes flew by so fast I thought it was five minutes."

This quiet place is covered over by thoughts and feelings that rush through the mind. In meditation you don't stop those thoughts and feelings, but you ask to be taken to a deeper place in yourself. Only in the place of peace can a person truly commune with God and with the soul. But even getting a bit closer to the soul brings a measure of peace, and you know it's real because it lasts.

TO LISTEN TO YOUR SOUL

As a boy, I remember being really jealous of the Old Testament prophets who got the word directly from God. I dreamed about hearing God's voice from the burning bush, like Moses. In my mind's eye I was walking with Athena, the Greek goddess of wisdom, at the battle of Troy, the way Achilles did. Then I grew up, and I found out that getting instructions from God, although it sounds great, doesn't happen too often. I'm not sure anymore what people mean by "the voice of God." Maybe it's just their conscience talking. Maybe it's a soothing voice they wish they could hear, and so they do.

But I am sure that spirit communicates with us. I would not personally call this speaking to God. I like the term *tuning in to your soul* better. The voice you hear is your own, but it comes from a deeper place than other voices. Most of the voices we hear in our head are echoes of things our parents told us, or old thoughts from the past that keep coming back: "You better not do *that* again." "Remember what happened the last time." "Uh-oh, here comes temptation."

The voice of your soul isn't the same old thing. It is always *now*. It gives you a fresh impulse to do something: "Oh, I never thought of that." "Do you see what I see?" "I really want to check that out." These don't seem like religious or holy thoughts. The soul doesn't have to sound like God speaking from a burning bush. It mostly isn't, at least not when I tune in. My soul is more interested in giving me a fresh start every day, in making my life new. Keeping it from being stale.

Instead of echoing the past, your soul wants you to feel alive right now, ready to try something new or feel something new.

Why not run for class president? Or try out for the cheerleading squad? Or join the debating team?

Listen to that song you love! Why not write your own?

Look at that gorgeous sunset! Why not take a really good photograph of it and develop the photo yourself?

Everyone has experienced what it's like to be bored by the same old things. You get up in the morning to the same breakfast, the same family, the same toothbrush. Yet there is a way that each day is fresh, or should be, as long as you tune in, because in truth every day *is* different. No two days are completely the same, and what makes them different is that you get new opportunities each day.

If you can see each day anew, you are tuned in to your soul. One could also call this having a telephone line to God, because God is the source of these new things that life brings us. To me, if you can see something new in the face of a person you love, or see the sunrise as new, or greet the day as if a whole new world is being born, you are listening to your soul. "Hearing God's voice" is another way of saying the same thing.

TO PROVIDE HIGHER VALUES

You've probably heard of Mother Teresa, the famous Catholic nun who traveled from Europe to India so that she could care for sick and starving children that nobody else wanted. Mother Teresa won the Nobel Peace Prize, but there's one thing most people don't know about this world-famous figure. A psychology professor once showed a film of her kissing and caring for babies, and everyone in the audience who watched the film experienced a physical change. Their immune system, the system that fights off illness, got stronger on the spot—within a few minutes a chemical called IgA increased in their bodies. Not that you need to know what IgA is. The point is that just looking at love in action makes your body stronger, less vulnerable to disease.

I find this amazing, all the more so because the people in the audience didn't even have to like Mother Teresa. Their bodies responded regardless of their opinions about her. The kind of love she displayed has been focused on God for centuries. God gives us the strength to act on our highest values. Love is one, but so are honor and truth and faith in goodness.

A soul is like a ship carrying precious cargo. But this cargo is invisible because it's your values, the things you live by. Here we are talking about really personal values. If you know that good is more powerful than evil, you've found a soul value. If you know that you will never die, that is another soul value. One of the most important reasons for being alive is to explore your own soul and discover these things for yourself. I would rather know in my heart of hearts that eternity is real than to read it from a great wise man.

God is where these soul values come from. I once read this wonderful sentence: "To be truly human, you have to go beyond the human." You're not going to get there by doing what everybody else does and only seeing what you're supposed to see. Look at your little brother slurping milk out of his cereal bowl. Can you see that he is totally unique in the universe?

WHAT THE SOUL CAN SEE

Look at your teacher scribbling words on the blackboard. Can you see that a soul is working out its deepest hopes and wishes?

Look at your coach shouting to get you to run downfield faster. Can you see that he is on the mysterious voyage of eternity?

I know all this sounds mystical, but it's also true. You see different things when you look through the eyes of the soul. The whole adventure of having a soul is to get beneath the surface. People try to be good because they think it brings them closer to God. I feel closer to God when I say to myself, "Open your eyes! There's a world you never imagined out there."

If God makes you want to live your vision, then he's doing his job. A spiritual vision of life might be one of the following:

- To feel God's presence personally

- To be united with God

- To feel what eternal love is like

- To live fully in the moment

- To find more beauty in the world every day

- To uncover a new truth every day

- To know yourself

- To touch the edge of eternity

- To be a child of the universe

This isn't just a hypothetical list. These are phrases young people actually tell me. For each of these visions, I know at least one teenager who is trying to live it out. And in every case I would call that person someone who has found the secret of happiness. Not just happiness for a day or a month, or happiness that lasts as long as everything is going your way, but deep happiness that satisfies the soul.

"Give Me Faith"

Q: **How do you get faith? I have born-again friends who tell me all the time that their life is "faith based." What do they mean?**

A: Faith is spiritual certainty. I think you're afraid you don't have enough of it because your friends seem to have more. Don't be discouraged. Faith doesn't come from never missing church. You don't need God to begin to have faith. Do you have faith that the sun will come up tomorrow? That gravity will still work? That your body will be healthy and sound? These are matters of faith that have nothing to do with spirit. They are more like trust. You trust your house to be there when you come home from school, but no one would say that this makes you a person of faith.

Faith goes beyond visible things. When you have trust in something you can't see, you are getting closer to faith. The most powerful electron microscope can't see electrons or quarks, but the mind knows they exist. Keep an open mind. Look for those moments when your trust in God or goodness or doing the right thing works out. That's how faith begins to grow.

But I don't want you to plunge into blind faith. Blind faith is stubborn certainty. Some people settle the whole question of faith in about ten minutes by saying, "I know God exists because that's what my religion says. The matter is closed." I would consider that a perfect example of blind faith. But there is a faith that opens your eyes, and that is the kind that God values most. If you take the time and look deep enough, I believe that all of the following would prove to be true:

Good is more powerful than evil.

All human beings are spiritual.

Intelligence has organized the universe.

The greatest force in nature is growth.

Infinite possibilities are always present.

Eternity can be found right now.

God is love.

Now, these are huge statements. Without exaggeration, it could take a lifetime to prove that they are true. Look upon them as articles of faith. You can believe in them and live them in your own life, even though you haven't totally proved them to yourself. So try this: Pick one thing from the list, such as "Good is more powerful than evil." Keep watch and notice all the good things in the world, like families and the love that they show, charities, volunteer work, altruism, heroism, friendship, and so on. Keep reminding yourself of how these good things have continued for centuries, even as wars rise and fall, dictators come and go, sickness and death abound. In the balance life is winning, and it's winning through our goodness.

NEGATIVE FAITH

Some people put their faith in negatives. They have faith in Murphy's Law, for example, which says that if something can go wrong, it will. They have faith that life is unfair. They have faith that human behavior is basically selfish. This kind of negative faith throws a dark cloud over their days. Yet negative faith isn't automatically true. You can't prove that things always go wrong or that life is unfair or that people always act selfishly. There is too much evidence on the other side. So why have faith in something that is unprovable and negative at the same time? In reality positive faith has endured for thousands of years, and if you remember just that one thing, I think your problem with faith will soon be over.

How Are Miracles Chosen?

Q: If God causes miracles, how does he choose who gets one?

A: I imagine you'd like to have a miracle of your own. We all would. I was watching TV a few years ago when I saw something amazing. A very sick man had traveled from Ireland to France, intending to bathe in the waters of a sacred healing spring. The spring is very famous. It is located in Lourdes and has many healings to its credit. The man arrived late and couldn't get in the gates, however, so he never got close to the waters that were supposed to heal him. All he could do was stand outside the walls and listen to the loudspeakers that were broadcasting evening services.

185

He went back to his hotel and lay down, feeling tired. His disease, which was multiple sclerosis (or MS), made him feel tired a lot of the time, and it was growing worse, year by year. Eventually it would prove fatal, as MS is incurable.

Suddenly, as he lay there, the man felt something unusual. His body grew hot, and with his inner eye he could see light inside himself. Both the heat and the light grew very intense, until he lost consciousness. A moment later he woke up, and he knew that his illness was gone. Medical tests proved that it was, and he entered the ranks of the small number of people who have been healed at Lourdes. They are a tiny number compared with the millions of pilgrims who ask for healing.

WHO GETS PICKED AND WHY?

Nobody knows, but I think miracles fit into a bigger picture. Whether you think of God as a higher power, a divine father, a protector, or any other conception, the world has witnessed too many miracles to doubt that they can occur. When they do, everybody benefits because each miracle is a reminder that something is beyond our world. That something is divine and holy. Sometimes it reaches into our physical world and gives us an example of what lies beyond our knowledge. A miracle wakes you up to a higher reality—walking on water, healing the sick through touch, spreading love by a single glance. I keep that in mind, and whenever I am disappointed that I didn't get my own personal miracle, I tell myself, "Every miracle happened for me already. I am rich in miracles, no matter what happens."

The Glue of the Universe

Q: What does God do? I mean, once he created the universe, wasn't he basically done?

A: Creation isn't just one step, like pulling a cake out of the oven. Right this second the universe is being created as new stars are born. Another part of the universe is holding still and changing only gradually, like the stars that were created billions of years ago. And a third part of the universe is breaking down, giving way to destruction, like the stars that explode into novas or collapse into black holes.

God is the power and intelligence behind all three. He upholds the creation. Not everybody loves this idea. In the age of science the universe isn't upheld by its creator. It is upheld by physical forces like gravity. To believe that God is waiting in the wings, like a choreographer running the show but never appearing on stage, is considered a religious belief, not science.

But I think there's a deeper science that still allows for God. On one level the whole universe looks like billions of galaxies tumbling out of control through space. The big bang blasted the universe into existence in a firestorm of incredible energy, without pattern or form. Is this all there is? If so, then one huge question cannot be answered: Why did life ever happen?

Go out and explode a firecracker on the Fourth of July. Wouldn't you be amazed to find out that it brought anything to life? Explosions blow things to bits. But the big bang didn't do that. It exploded with a force billions of times more powerful than all the firecrackers and bombs on Earth, yet this delicate strand called DNA was born out of it just as stars and galaxies were. To me, the notion that DNA could just appear randomly out of swirling energy is not believable. Each bit of human DNA is made up of three billion tiny chemical pairs linked in perfect order. Move a few thousand to a new place and you get a totally different person. Move 1 percent out of place and you get a mountain gorilla instead of a human being.

Saying DNA is an accident is like saying I could write the dictionary by throwing a Scrabble game up in the air and letting the letters fall where they may.

A much better explanation is that intelligence is at work. This intelligence upholds the universe by creating images. Your body is an image of this intelligence. So is everyone else you know, each image being slightly different from every other. God's purpose in upholding the universe is like the purpose of anyone who is looking in a mirror. He wants to see what he looks like. Except that in this case, since God's intelligence is infinite, he needs infinite images to see himself. And that is what the universe is and always has been: the mirror of infinity.

Why Doesn't God Step In?

Q: Why does God allow bad things to happen? Couldn't he just step in and fix them?

A: Only in a different world would God step in. That kind of a world would not have free will in it. In this world we are all free to choose. Bad things happen because of wrong choices a lot of the time. If you go rock climbing without safety equipment, that is your choice. But you might fall, and if you do, God won't be there to catch you in midair.

Freedom of choice is not just a rule set up for humans. If you look around, you will see that animals and plants are also free. A seed from a maple tree gets blown by the wind, and where it lands isn't always the right place for it. Sometimes it lands on harsh ground where nothing can grow. Sometimes it lands on fertile ground where it will grow perfectly. In a different world every seed might find the perfect way to grow. But in this one nature explodes in a million directions, and some creatures perish while others survive.

IS THIS FAIR?

Couldn't God have set up creation so that there would be no pain and suffering at all? Of course. If you go out among the stars, immense galaxies are born and die without the slightest pain. On our home planet pain isn't part of the rain or the sun. Pain is more personal than that. For you and me and everyone we know, both bad things and good things are part of the package. Light and dark, good and evil, are constantly at play. God's purpose was to set the stage for us and then to allow us to create anything we wanted. If you and I ever get to see another world—perhaps the world of the angels—we will find proof that only good can exist. For now this world of light and dark is the gift we have received from the creator.

Where Did I Sin?

Q: I come from a strict religious background where bad people are punished for their sins. But how do you know when you have sinned? I have had bad things happen to me, and I don't remember doing anything wrong.

A: I think you have spotted a big weakness in the whole theory of sin. It doesn't seem like such a good system if people are punished for things they can't remember doing. I don't remember stepping on an anthill recently, but to some faiths it is a sin to kill even the smallest being. I don't remember accidentally saying a lot of things that may have hurt someone's feelings. Is that a tiny sin or a middle-size one?

It would be even worse if the wrong people were being punished. When a jet plane crashes and everyone is killed, it's hard to believe that God looked down and decided that all one hundred passengers were guilty of sin and deserved to die.

SIN IS A PUZZLE

I am not sure there's a good way out of this problem. Wise men have tried to solve it for thousands of years. The best answer, for me at least, is to stop thinking that God punishes us at all. You already know when you are doing something bad. Your conscience tells you. Part of growing up is to listen to that conscience. If you feel guilty about something, go and correct it. Do what it takes until the guilt is gone. In that way you won't have to worry about waiting for God to punish you. As long as you balance your life so that there is far more good in it than bad, sin becomes much less important. What's really important is growing in your soul day by day. Focus your attention there and let the heavy religious thinkers fret about the theory of sin without you. They are going to anyway.

Original Sin

Q: **What about the Garden of Eden? I was taught that Adam and Eve sinned, and that is why we have so much suffering now.**

A: The story of the Garden of Eden poses a question: Is everyone a sinner because sometime in the deep past our ancestors were sinners? People have answered this question with both yes and no. There is no one certain answer. This may surprise you, but billions of people have never heard the story of Adam and Eve. It isn't part of their spiritual tradition, and therefore they have never understood why the Garden of Eden is so important. They don't feel like the children of original sin. Original sin is the name given to the disobedience that Adam and Eve showed toward God. For their disobedience they were driven from the Garden of Eden, and from that time on, human beings have sinned and suffered.

One thing is certain. Everyone makes mistakes, and everyone has more bad things happen to them than they would like. Whether you believe in the story of the Garden of Eden or not, reducing the suffering in your life is important. In fact, that is the whole point of being spiritual: You can find a way to leave suffering behind.

God Is Watching

Q: **Does God watch everything I do? That makes me feel that I could be punished just for my thoughts or that I will never be good enough to satisfy him.**

A: It's very hard for most people to think about God except as a human being sitting on a throne in the clouds. This kind of God is said to look down and watch everything in creation. He knows who has been good and who has been bad, and we are all judged accordingly. But what if God is everywhere? Then he can't be sitting outside the game watching it. He is part of every person, and also part of every action, both good and bad. It's harder to imagine God that way, but I think it's closer to the truth. God is watching you because you are watching yourself. When you have a thought, so does God. When you take a cookie from the cookie jar without permission, so does God.

DOES THAT SOUND STRANGE?

We don't think of God's taking a cookie from the cookie jar. Maybe we should, because the idea of a punishing God sitting up on his throne is very intimidating. Getting away from God as the great judge in the sky is a challenge for millions of people who would rather believe in a God that acts like a human being who likes some things and dislikes others. I think God sees everything and accepts everything. That is what makes him God. Part of you is just like that. It sees everything about you and accepts all of it. In your spiritual life you will be trying to reclaim that part of yourself, which is your soul. You will not worry about someone in the sky passing judgment on you, because you will see yourself as a unique part of the divine creation, and therefore as of infinite value. You are worth as much to God as he is worth to himself.

McDonald's in Heaven?

Q: Is there a McDonald's in heaven?

A: I must tell you that this isn't a question anybody has ever asked me—I read it in a book I picked up at the airport. But since it was a question asked by a teenager, I began to think about it. And to my surprise, I had to admit that my answer wasn't either yes or no. A lot of people want the answer to be yes, because they think of heaven as having all the best things here on Earth, and for them a McDonald's (or a Wendy's or a really good ice cream stand) belongs in heaven.

HEAVEN IS FOR YOU

But my answer is that heaven contains what you want it to. You may find it hard to believe, but I think everyone gets the heaven that matches their imagination. What is heaven but a place where what you deeply love comes true? God doesn't force you to love one thing or another—it's your choice. Maybe you love hot dogs and hate fish, while someone else has the opposite tastes. Heaven isn't a place with fixed scenery. It's the essence of God's love. And I think that essence can take any form. That is why every mother sees her own baby as beautiful, because the essence of love is found in her baby. Heaven for each of us will take the shape that brings out what we love and what we see as perfect.

Does God Love Me?

Q: How do I know that God loves me? There are a lot of times when I don't love myself.

A: This is a sensitive question because we all have moments when we don't love ourselves. It's attractive to think that at least God must love us, but then there is that speck of doubt. After all, if he knows me better than I know myself, maybe he doesn't love me at all. Maybe he has ticked off a list of my bad qualities and

I just don't stack up as all that lovable. I think you can put that worry away. God exists at the level of your soul. They are both made of the same thing, which is pure love. I would never put anyone down because they had a different notion of God. Maybe to them God does sit back and decide who is lovable and who isn't.

But for thousands of years spiritual people have said, "Love must come from somewhere. It is such a powerful feeling here on Earth that it seems to come from God." In your life you will experience moments of intense love, and then this idea of divine love will make sense. You will feel in your heart that you have touched God's love or that it is touching you. Without such an experience, I guess this whole question is kind of theoretical. God's love is empty until it is felt. But keep believing in love wherever it comes from, and one day I'm sure you will have such an experience. It exists everywhere, waiting to be recognized.

Waiting for God

Q: **Don't some people wait for God all their life and never meet him?**

A: Yes. But imagine that you went to a baseball game and you met someone sitting in the stands dressed in a uniform. This person says, "I want to be a good baseball player, so I am sitting here waiting until that happens." Such an attitude makes no sense. You can't sit on the sidelines and wait. That's fine if you want to be a spectator, but not if you want to play. God is pure creation. He is all game, and many would say he is all play. If you sit and wait, so does God. But if you get into the game, then every day brings a chance to meet God. God is in the next great idea you have, in the next burst of joy, in the next thing you suddenly love, no matter what that might be. God is the inner life of everything, not the outer mask. So if you plunge deep into any experience you love, eventually your love will take you to that place where you meet the source of love, which is God.

What Does God Look Like?

Q: I've seen paintings that are supposed to be true images of God. Are these what God looks like?

A: God has appeared in millions of images over the centuries. Although many people cherish an image of God as a loving father (usually with a white beard), there are equally loved images of God as a mother. But all of these are human images. What if I changed your question into this: What does love look like? Love doesn't have one face, and we don't expect it to. Love can be in a sunset, in a mother's smile, in music, or just in a beautiful feeling. God can't really be caught in images either, but we keep trying because that's one way to express worship and reverence. Enjoy the images that appeal to you, but also keep in mind that no single image will ever bring you the real thing.

Is God a Superstition?

Q: What's the difference between believing in God and believing in a superstition like Friday the thirteenth?

A: Superstitions wear out pretty quickly once you test them. There are usually several Friday the thirteenths a year, and bad things don't happen on them any more than on any other day. People who live around black cats don't have worse luck than people who don't. God has been called a superstition. When science was making its greatest advances, around the time of Einstein, many people thought that God would never survive the scientific worldview, since science deals in things you can see and touch. But God has survived, and Einstein himself believed that the most fascinating thing he could do with his own life was to keep trying to find out what was in the mind of God.

I think that's a wonderful attitude. The more you look for a divine intelligence in the universe, the more you find evidence of the things God stands for: order, creativity, omnipresence, infinity, eternity. Science sees all these things in the cosmos, and the other qualities of God—love, truth, compassion, joy—are left to us to search for as individuals, following our own heart for a lifetime. This is the great journey of the soul that I believe we were all born to follow.

Ticket to Heaven

Q: If I don't believe in God, can I still go to heaven?

A: No one can answer that with certainty, but you bring up a point that's really important. Believing in God could be a ticket to heaven, or maybe not. Just as not believing in God could keep you out of heaven, or maybe not. But God is more than a ticket to a better place after you die. God is part of you through your soul, and by exploring that part of you every day in some small way, you add to your life. This life is improved by getting to know your soul. What happens later will always be an open question. But if you only use God as a ticket to heaven, you will miss out on a lot here and now.

Life After Death

Q: Do you personally believe there is life after death? I am afraid of dying, and I am most afraid that I will just disappear forever.

A: I felt exactly the same way as a teen, which for many people is the most intense time for worrying about death. This is the time when answers that may work for a child no longer do. That's because you are beginning to think for yourself in a deeper way. And I hope you continue. I have met many adults who "know for sure" that death is the end of things or who "know for sure" that there is life after death.

I don't know for sure.

All I can say is that for me personally, all evidence is in favor of life after death. The entire universe displays intelligence, power, and organization. Life is shaped by an infinite creative force. Death occupies an honorable place inside this scheme. Every atom that once existed in someone's body is part of the life I now enjoy. With every breath I take in millions of atoms from someone who lived before me. My food comes from the earth, whose fertility is entirely due to past life forms.

DEATH IS NOT YOUR ENEMY

This means that death isn't the enemy of life. It serves life. It balances creation so that the universe doesn't fall into total stagnation. If stars didn't die, if plants didn't decompose, if whole ages didn't rise and fall, you wouldn't be here to read this page. Your very body depends on death, since millions of cells die every day to produce new tissue (if you looked at household dust under a microscope, you'd see that up to half of it consists of discarded skin cells that people slough off).

So nature is at ease with death. Why aren't we? Because our minds explore possibilities raised by fear. We are afraid to see our bodies grow old and come to an end. We therefore adopt the fear that our personalities will come to an end, and maybe our very selves will too. What worked for me was to keep asking about these possibilities but to get rid of the fear. When Socrates was about to die, having drunk the poison that the judges of Athens had condemned him to, his pupils wept to think that such a great philosopher and an innocent man should die. But Socrates was amazingly calm. He'd been taking a small step toward death every day, he explained. Why should the last one make him afraid?

I don't know if Socrates had the answer to your question, but he did find out how to end fear. Life and death are walking together, and you don't have to be afraid as you join their walk. As you mature, keep gaining in power and intelligence. All kinds of fears will drop away, and one day you will find that in your heart of hearts you have built a deep faith in these things. The closer you get to your source, which is pure power and intelligence, the easier it is to believe that life goes on eternally. In that belief you will understand that life after death isn't important. Life and death are important together, here and now.

Is Hell Real?

Q: I just found out that some religions don't believe in a hell after you die. But if hell is real, doesn't every person go there who is bad?

A: The existence of heaven and hell has not been a constant over the centuries. Throughout history many saints and sages have had visions of both, but of course no one can truly know if either one exists. (It's interesting that when people come back from near-death experiences, such as being resuscitated from a heart attack, they often speak of being drawn by a white light. In almost every case this light feels as if it is a loving light that leads to heaven. Only a tiny percentage of near-death experiences bring the feeling of hell.)

THE DEVIL'S DRAMA

Hell is very dramatic, with its pits of fire and devils. But remember that these are just images, and mostly they came from the imaginations of artists. Fear of punishment after death was once a major part of religious teaching in many countries. I don't think it needs to be, however, and whenever I meet people who have stopped being afraid of hell, I feel encouraged that spirituality based on love rather than fear is gaining ground. It's much more important to try to improve the huge suffering brought about by violence, crime, starvation, disease, and poverty around the world. The victims of these terrible things are already in a kind of hell that we can help them to escape. Devote yourself to creating a moment of heaven for someone here on Earth, rather than worrying about something that will never be proved.

How to See an Angel

Q: I love angels, and I was wondering if there is a way to see one. I have read in books that angels have been seen thousands of times in many cultures. Is that still possible?

A: It would be wonderful if angel-watching were like bird-watching. But angels seem to appear when the time is right and only then. I have met people who tell me that they were visited by an angel. Nobody, as far as I know, was actually looking for one. It just appeared, but each time there was some kind of important message—of either hope or healing—that the person received. You may already know that the word *angel* comes from the Greek word for *messenger.* Maybe that's the most important clue to how one might see an angel. If you are in need of a message from your soul, sometimes an angel will deliver it. But your soul has many other messages to deliver to you, so don't wait for an angel, but be on the lookout yourself. Be your own angel and discover what your soul wants to tell you.

Guardian Angels

Q: What does my guardian angel do? Can I connect with it?

A: Some people feel that they are very connected to a guardian. They feel a presence that protects and guides them in times of need. Their guardian angel isn't a person, but more like an inner voice that says, "Make this choice. It's better for you." So whenever these people resist doing what they know is bad, they will give the credit to the guardian angel that showed them how to make the right choice.

Can you also connect with your own guardian angel in this

way? I would not doubt it, since people are capable of all kinds of sensitivity—maybe one day you will be aware of a presence that guides and protects you. To me, it is even more important to be aware of your own inner nature. Have you ever been in a situation of danger that you escaped without knowing how you did it? Perhaps you were almost in a car accident or, without thinking, stepped off the curb in front of a bus. Just in time you swerved or pulled back. People who believe in guardian angels would say that it was the angel who protected them, but it is just as valid to say that we all see and feel more than we realize. Some part of you sees beyond your five senses. Consciously you may not have seen the reckless driver or the oncoming bus, but some part of you did. Whether you call this your angel or your own higher self doesn't matter. What does matter is to trust that you have a higher self that knows a lot about life and wants to connect with you.

Will I See God?

Q: When I die, will I see God personally?

A: The promise that we will all see God when we die is a source of great comfort and joy to hosts of people. Can anyone verify that it is true? I think this is a matter of faith, and in my experience, what you put your faith in, if you believe deeply, usually does come true.

God's Truth

Q: How should I respond when other kids say that everything in the Bible is true?

A: You want to answer with integrity and yet not offend them, since arguments over someone's religion never lead to a good ending. Agree that the Bible is one way that God's truth has been expressed. But it isn't the only truth, since there are many hundreds of scriptures that also contain the same truths expressed in other ways. If everyone could honor everyone else's faith, the world would be saved from a huge amount of violence and warfare. If your friends try to argue that only one faith and one scripture is true, don't be intimidated. They are reinforcing the age-old religious intolerance that has brought immense misery to human beings. You can still be their friend without joining in. In this case, by not arguing, you are adding to the peace in the world.

Turning the Other Cheek

Q: Does turning the other cheek mean that if someone hurts me once, I should let them hurt me twice? I have a hard time with this one. My natural urge is to hit back.

A: Turning the other cheek is about not returning violence with violence. It's normal that when someone hurts you, your first impulse may be to hit back. That's the basic reaction of small children, and many people grow up trying hard to overcome it when they are adults. Nations fight because the spiritual value of being nonviolent hasn't sunk in. You don't have to let someone hurt you twice. Nobody wants you to become a victim. But if you can learn to resist your own impulse to hurt them back, you will become one of the peacemakers in the world. Peace begins one person at a time, and you can become such a person, starting today.

Afraid of God?

Q: If God is going to punish us for being bad, shouldn't we be afraid of him? I'm mostly afraid of God, even though I know I am supposed to love him.

A: Being afraid of God goes along with the whole notion of sin. If you see God as a punisher, it's only natural to be afraid. Since many people also believe that they are sinners, this makes fear of God almost impossible to escape. My belief is that you don't need a punishing God for any reason. You can pray to God as your consoler, protector, best friend, soul mate, divine father or mother—there are so many faces to God, without having to look at him as an angry, punishing deity.

POSTSCRIPT

For Ever and Ever

As a boy in India, I went to a school run by the
Christian Brothers. I wasn't a Christian myself; neither were most
of the other boys in my classes. But our teachers were. Many, as I
remember, came from Ireland, a place so far away I could never
imagine visiting it.

So there I was, a small brown boy learning the Lord's Prayer
from very devout, very pale Catholics. I'd bow my head and mur-
mur those familiar words: "For thine is the kingdom, and the
power, and the glory, for ever and ever. Amen."

Beautiful words, but did I believe them? Well, the kingdom
part didn't strike the right chord because in 1945, right before I
was born, India had gained freedom from an English king. "The
power, and the glory" sank in. It took twenty-five years, but eventually I came to see that the best way to live your life is to pursue the invisible power and glory that is present everywhere in the
universe.

Which leaves the last four words: "for ever and ever."

They stand for eternity, and eternity is the biggest concept
anyone could hope to explore. Here we are, you and I, at the end
of a journey, yet as far as the eye can see, eternity stretches, as
vast in front of us as behind us. Which means we aren't ever at
the end of our journey. No matter how young you are, you have

eternity to go. No matter how old you are, you have eternity to go. Eternity is the great equalizer. It's not how good or bad you are that makes you equal in the eyes of God. Rather, it's how far into eternity you've come.

Eternity is the school of life. Even if you believe that life began only two billion years ago on Earth, even if you believe that the universe was born fifteen billion years ago in the big bang, eternity isn't shaken. At the deepest level of nature time disappears. There is only eternity left when all the matter and energy have gone *poof*! The miracle is that you can visit this timeless place. I'm inviting you to go there with me—with everyone, if they want to come too.

My last word to you is that you deserve eternity, and you deserve the power and glory that come with it. All three exist here and now. There's no waiting around. You have everything you need for the trip:

You can think.

You can feel.

You can do.

Turn these everyday things toward the far horizon of your deepest dreams, and you will soon be in pursuit of eternity. Look for me. I will be just ahead of you, or perhaps just behind. In any event, we will recognize each other.

We're the ones who still have eternity to go.